The Thackerays in India

Owing to the antiquity and rarity of this book, certain pages are regrettably absent, and readability is compromised due to the blurring of the original text. If you possess any insights regarding the availability of these missing sections, kindly inform us. Your assistance is crucial in ensuring the completion of this significant work for the benefit of future generations.

The Thackerays in India

AND SOME CALCUTTA GRAVES

BY SIR WILLIAM WILSON HUNTER,
K.C.S.I., M.A., LL.D.

GYAN

Published by

Gyan Publishing House
5, Ansari Road
Daryaganj, New Delhi-110002
Phone: 011-47034999, 9811692060
E-mail: books@gyanbooks.com

Distribution Network
gyanbooks.com
India, USA, Canada, UK, Australia

ISBN: 978-93-6208-109-4 (HB)
First Published, 1897

2nd Impression 2024

Printed at: Gyan Press, Delhi.

THE THACKERAYS IN INDIA
Author: SIR WILLIAM WILSON HUNTER

The Thackerays in India

The Thackerays in India

AND SOME CALCUTTA GRAVES

By SIR WILLIAM WILSON HUNTER, K.C.S.I., M.A., LL.D.

HENRY FROWDE, LONDON: 1897

TO MY DEAR WIFE

I DEDICATE THIS BOOK

First Edition, January 1897: 5000 *copies.*

CONTENTS

PAGE

CHAP. I.—SOME CALCUTTA GRAVES 9

CHAP. II.—THACKERAY'S GRANDFATHER IN BENGAL . 63

CHAP. III.—THACKERAY'S UNCLES IN INDIA . . . 111

CHAP. IV.—THACKERAY'S FATHER IN BENGAL. . . 141

THE THACKERAYS IN INDIA

CHAPTER I

SOME CALCUTTA GRAVES

'It is said that the last descendant of Milton died a parish clerk in Calcutta.' At least so wrote the easy-going biographer in the Chandos edition, and not having my Masson at hand, it did not occur to me that for Calcutta one should read Madras. The careless rumour set me wandering for a few evenings among the old burial-grounds of the city, to see if perchance I might come on the grandson of that youngest daughter Deborah whom Milton loved.

The great magazines of mortality upon the outskirts of Calcutta were explored in vain. Gradually, however, in pacing up and down their thick-set avenues of tombs, the parish clerk was crowded out of my mind by the long procession of well-known Indian names: some of them ennobled by heroic deeds, some mutely protesting against unmerited obloquy, not a few tarnished by greed and crime, but all pleading the pardon that is earned by death.

Most mournful of graveyards are those walled-up ghostly settlements, desolate spaces of brick ruins and blotched plaster, reproachful of forgetfulness and neglect. It was difficult to restrain some retrospective pity for the inmates of the squalid tenements —for their hard, hot lives more than a hundred years ago, solaced by none of the alleviations which have become the necessaries of our modern Indian existence; with few airy verandas or lofty ceilings, without punkahs, without ice, without the possibility of change to the hills, or respite to their exile by visits home. The mental stagnation of a small society given to arrack punch and heavy dinners in the heat of the tropical day, and dependent for their news from the outer world on three or four shipments a year, produced a *tedium vitae* even harder to bear. 'The waste of spirits in this cursed country,' cries Sir Philip Francis, the man of all others best fitted to bear up against the malady, 'is a disease unconquerable, a misery unutterable.' If the world dealt hardly with them in life, it has made no amends to their memory. As I thought of how much they achieved, and how little they have been honoured, I found myself involuntarily composing an apologia for the dead.

The English drama in India is played amid a bustle of exits and entrances, and a hurried scene-shifting, which allow time for nothing but the present. Migratory Calcutta takes knowledge only of the people with whom it dances and dines, and regards all others, who do not go out, with an unconcern quite good natured but absolutely complete. Now the dwellers in these silent settlements have not gone out anywhere for a century. They have sat at no man's feast nor heard any church-bell knoll, and the most famous of them, under their pyramidal tombs, are objects of as genteel an indifference to Calcutta as is the half-pagan population fallen away from Christian rites in the slums of the city. History, too, turns from them with an averted eye. They took part in great events and left a rich inheritance to the nation. But they did so amid a furious cross-fire of invective that leaves for many of them only the choice between infamy and oblivion.

It was their hard destiny to make, unloved, an empire. The rude conflict of interests at home and in India, amid which that empire was reared, allowed little chance of fair treatment to the builders, with their sword in one hand and the trowel in the other. The slanders of the last century still putrefy in a mass of Reflections and Considerations and British Museum tracts. Caraccioli's *Life of Clive* forms a good foul specimen of their dregs, and Macaulay's story of Warren Hastings' parentage an iridescent bubble from their scum.

Yet to these poor predecessors of ours, who lived and died at their work, and to whom fame was always half disfame, we owe no small debt. They found Calcutta a swamp, and they created on it a capital. They are reproached for the superfluity of mosquito-breeding ponds and cholera-haunted tanks which they scattered over the town. But we forget that much of Calcutta was then a marsh, amid which its builders had to dig wide, deep holes, so as to get a little earth with which, like beavers, they might pile up dry spots for their dwellings. The excavations that yielded the raised mounds for their homes upon an almost fluid ooze, are the mosquito-breeding ponds of to-day. We are apt to forget, too, the price paid for Calcutta by past generations of Englishmen; that, in fact, our City of Palaces is circumvallated by entrenchments of their dead.

In the South Park Street graveyard, that aceldama of ancient animosities, how many fierce passions have been shovelled underground! It was opened in 1767, just before the final struggle by which England declared that India should be thenceforward not alone the concern of the Company, but also of the nation. The blundering ignorance with which Parliament gave effect to this righteous resolve formed one of the many dangers that British rule in India has survived, almost in spite of the rulers. Instead of sending out a Governor-General to take command in the joint names of the Company and the Crown, Parliament retained the Company's Governor, Warren Hastings, and sent out a Council to override him by a majority of votes.

Of the three councillors thus despatched to Bengal, two had no experience in civil administration, the third has come down in history as the most malignant Englishman of that age. If any doubt still exists as to the identity of Francis with Junius in England, he stands revealed as an unabashed Junius in Bengal—a Junius set free from the fear of the pillory, and with his ears safe from the hangman's knife.

Philip Francis sailed for India with a sore heart. Notwithstanding his cleverness as an official and the terrible power of his pen, he found himself a failure in English political life. He had lost money by speculating in the public funds, he had thrown up his War Office appointment in chagrin at being superseded, the two final letters of Junius had fallen flat. The Indian Council opened to him possibilities of a new and higher flight. He was still young, exactly thirty-four years of age, when he landed at Calcutta in October, 1774. The two colleagues who accompanied him were soldiers of fashion, and indeed of merit. But Francis felt that in his administrative ambitions he could use them as tools. They were elderly men, as age was then reckoned in the Indian official world. General Clavering was fifty-two, and Colonel Monson forty-four. Francis hoped with good reason to outlive them both.

Of the two other councillors awaiting them in India, one was the Governor-General, Warren Hastings, who entered the Company's service as far back as 1750, and whose retirement seemed in 1774 a question of five years at the utmost. The second, Barwell, son of a former Governor of Bengal, had made a rapid fortune, and although only thirty-three years of age, he longed to enjoy it in England. Francis looked on himself as the residuary legatee of the powers wielded by his four colleagues. Shortly after his arrival in Calcutta he wrote with characteristic arrogance of 'this glorious Empire which I was sent to save and govern.' As he wound his meshes round Hastings he took a more confident tone. 'I am now, I think, on the road to the Government of Bengal, which I believe is the first situation in the world attainable by a subject. I will not balk my future.'

Francis found, however, that in order to oust Warren Hastings, he must first ruin him. During the twenty-one years' combat which followed, he exhausted every resource of incrimination and intrigue. His correspondence was a long libel against the man whose destruction he sought, at times rising to shrieks of malevolence. 'The Court of Directors is devoted to Hastings,' he wrote, 'and I am in hopes will go to the devil with him.' One by one his poisoned darts fell blunted off the armour of quiet persistence which Hastings opposed to all attacks. But in 1774 Francis started with everything in his favour—the promise of the future which belongs to youth, and in the present the power of crushing the Governor-General by the votes of himself and his two military allies in Council.

The first act of the drama extended over six years, and closed in 1780 with the retreat of Francis to England; outmanœuvred in Council; beaten at his own weapon, the pen; leaving his two allies in their graves; and carrying on his body the mark of Hastings' pistol-shot. The second act lasted fifteen years, and ended in 1795 with the acquittal of Hastings on every charge by the House of Lords. The active vendetta against him then ceased, leaving to his enemies the pangs of disappointed hatred.

But the curtain finally fell on a more imposing scene, after Francis *aeternum servans sub pectore vulnus* had dropped out of public life, when in 1813 the House of Commons rose in honour of the great Governor-General, and stood bare-headed as Warren Hastings passed forth.

The South Park Street burial-ground supplies the necrology of the first or Calcutta act of this long drama. There rests Sir John Clavering, the irate Commander-in-Chief, who in his duel with a colleague in Council, Barwell, was with difficulty withdrawn from the ground, furiously calling for another shot. It is due to Barwell to add that this demand arose solely from the extreme pugnacity of the general. Clavering had wanted to fight the Duke of Richmond for words used in public debate before he left England, and he nearly fought Warren Hastings in India. At one crisis, indeed, it seemed as if he would array the military forces against the civil government in Bengal. On hearing of Hastings' conditional resignation, Sir John Clavering instantly declared himself Governor-General, and demanded the keys of the Fort. It was only the firm calm of Hastings, backed by the Supreme

Court, that averted a collision between the civil and the military powers. The poor passionate knight has lain very quiet since one sweltering afternoon in August, 1777, when, writes Francis, 'after a delirium of many hours [he] expired at half-past two p.m., and was buried at eight. The Governor ordered minute guns.'

A year previously the other ally of Francis, Colonel Monson, had been borne to the same graveyard. Monson suffered miseries from the climate since the day he reached India, and was soon forced to fly to sea to save his life. Two years after his arrival he resigned his office, sorely stricken with disease. But before he could escape to England, death clutched him. In September, 1776, they buried him in a nameless grave, beside that of his wife, Lady Anne, who had died in the preceding February.

They lie separately but close together in the South Park Street burial-ground, in two long graves covered with crumbling arched brickwork, over which no inscription was ever placed. Clavering's tomb stands hard by.

The Lady Anne Monson felt that she was much

too good for Indian society, being in fact a daughter of the Earl of Darlington, and a great grand-daughter of Charles II by Barbara Villiers. But she consoled herself for her uncourtly surroundings by whist parties that led the fashion in Calcutta. She herself was a superior player, and it was at her house that Francis began his whist winnings, which, as he tells a friend in 1776, 'on one blessed day of the present year of our Lord' amounted to £20,000.

It was Lady Anne, too, who set afloat the story that Warren Hastings 'was the natural son of a steward of her father's.' One might have thought that the remembrance of her own slip in life would have warned her off such dangerous ground. But if the men of that wrathful age lied about their opponents, the ladies fibbed with a subtler venom. Nor was her slander more audacious than the falsehood to which Macaulay has put the seal of history. Macaulay informs us that Hastings' father, 'an idle, worthless boy, married before he was sixteen, lost his wife in two years, and died in the West Indies.' The parish registers and Oxford lists prove that the 'idle, worthless boy' was an ordained clergyman, educated at Balliol College, and twenty-four or twenty-six years of age when he married his wife, who was herself twenty-five.

The legend lives, and will live, in the picturesque pages of Macaulay, whose dangerous gift it was to equally take captive his readers whether he were right or wrong. His genius embedded in amber a calumny that would otherwise have died a natural death. Whatever were the failings or misfortunes of Hastings' father, they were the failings and misfortunes of an educated grown-up man. Sixteen months of the Calcutta climate silenced Lady Anne Monson's backbiting for ever. 'After lying speechless through the day,' writes Francis' secretary on February 18, 1776, 'she departed last night about ten.' The poor lady has talked no scandal since.

The secretary of Francis was his brother-in-law; brother of that faithful wife whom Francis left in England, and to whom he proved so false. This retainer also fell a victim to the climate, without even the empty honour of a tomb in the Calcutta necropolis. In November, 1776, the secretary fled to sea in hope of recovery, but only to find a grave on the solitary Ganjam coast. Within three years after Francis landed under the guns of Fort William, confident that he held the reversion of India, death had stripped him of the last of his allies, and he stood at bay, alone. It was the memory of these Indian graves, and of the bullet which he put into Francis' right side, that stirred Hastings to his stern summary of the struggle: 'My antagonists sickened, died, and fled.'

In the South Park Street burial-ground also lies Colonel Pearse, who acted as second to Warren Hastings in his duel with Francis. Colonel Pearse pleasantly records that he found 'the gentlemen were both unacquainted with the modes usually observed on those occasions.' But if the combatants asked questions of ignorance, they had a very clear idea as to what they had come to do in that jungle-lane. There is, indeed, something above the passions of humanity in Hastings' quiet resolve to bring the anarchy to an end. On July 3, 1780, he wrote a Minute which charged Francis with treachery and falsehood in regard to the Maratha War. 'I judge of his public conduct by my experience of his private, which I have found void of truth and honour. This is a severe charge, but temperately and deliberately made,' he added, to leave no option as to the result.

The same day, however, Francis took to bed with fever, and for six weeks Hastings kept his Minute loaded to the muzzle in his desk. On August 14, 1780, Francis having recovered, Hastings politely sent him a copy of it, to avoid anything like a scene at the meeting of Council next forenoon. When they reached the ground three mornings afterwards, Hastings objected to fourteen paces —adopted on the precedent of the late Fox and Adam duel in England—as being 'a great distance for pistols.' Himself nothing of a marksman, he let Francis deliberately raise his weapon 'three times to the present.' When it missed fire, he waited till it was freshly primed, and again allowed his adversary the first shot. Hastings then fired. 'Mr. Francis staggered,' wrote Colonel Pearse, 'and in attempting to sit down, he fell and said he was a dead man. Mr. Hastings, hearing this, cried out, "Good God, I hope not!" and immediately went up to him.'

Francis was not killed. But a few months later his broken health drove him home to England, where he lived a life of active malevolence for thirty-eight more years. He died quietly in his sleep at the age of seventy-eight. In the same year, 1818, Warren Hastings passed painfully away, aged eighty-six. Colonel Pearse, his second in the duel, with an heroic record of Guadaloupe, Havanna, Belleisle, and the Carnatic, did not live to go home. He was buried in Calcutta in 1789, 'the senior officer of the Bengal army,' at the age of forty-seven.

In the fierce struggles of the pent-up stifling Settlement, no reputation was too high, no fate too tragic, to escape the ravening tusk of slander. How these poor dead people hated their great men! They stoned their prophets: to be mentioned was to be defamed. It is with a sense of relief that we turn from what was said about the founders of the British power in India to what they did. Whatever their failings or their falsehoods, the libellers and the libelled dwell very quietly with each other now. The defamed lie as cool as their defamers. If our Calcutta graveyards are not temples of reconciliation, they are at least sanctuaries of silence. And, alike for some hard, mean ambitions which they cover over, and for some noble names done to dishonour by slanderous tongues, perhaps silence is most merciful. Here they fear no more the heat of the sun, falsehood and censure rash come not near them, and in place of the sharp bitings of malice they have but to encounter the toothless maw of the worm.

How much of the fierce invective of that age are we to believe? We must remember that it was the age in which Mr. Batson struck Warren Hastings in the Council Chamber with his fist. It was also the age in which a Governor of Madras, Lord Pigot, snatched away a mutinous resolution from his colleagues in Council, suspended them from office, ordered the arrest of the commander of the troops, was himself seized by the military, and died in confinement.

'I will not content myself,' wrote Francis of the great Commander-in-Chief who came after Clavering, 'with saying I never knew, but upon my soul I never heard of, so abandoned a scoundrel. It is a character to which your English ideas of dirt and meanness do not reach. Nor is it to be met with even in Bengal: even here it excites execration and contempt.' Shall we accept these words as a fair portrait of the warrior-statesman before whose monument in Westminster Abbey, with its figures of Victory and a conquered Province, many a young soldier has paused to read a nation's record of the services of Sir Eyre Coote?

Barwell, as we saw, escaped the bullet of Clavering. He went home to pose as a nabob for a quarter of a century in Sussex, and to order round 'more curricles.' But the pistols of Honourable Members of Council in the last century were less deadly than their pens. They safely stabbed each other in their diaries, and poignarded their enemies in letters to England. If Barwell passed scathless through the fire of one colleague, he fell a victim to a 'private memorandum' of another. 'Mr. Barwell, I think,' wrote Francis, 'has all the bad qualities common to this climate and country, of which he is in every sense a native; but I do not affirm that there is no mixture whatsoever of good in his composition. He is rapacious without industry, and ambitious without an exertion of his faculties or steady application to affairs. He will do whatever can be done by bribery and intrigue. He has no other resource.'

What degree of verisimilitude shall we credit to these appalling silhouettes of darkest shadow? Barwell seems to have been in truth a greedy and pompous person. But if one memory could have been spared, it might surely have been that of Admiral Watson, who brought succour to the Settlement in its dire extremity after the Black Hole. How dire was that extremity it is now difficult to realize. All through the rains of 1756 our hapless refugees from Calcutta were huddled together at Fulta in the fever-stricken delta; a crowd of haggard white men and despairing white women with their skeleton children, in boats or straw hovels, dependent for their daily food on the pity of the natives; 'clad in the meanest apparel,' writes an eye-witness, 'and for almost five months surrounded by sickness and disease.' They sank so low as to approve 'a complimentary letter' to the Prince who had driven them forth and suffocated their countrymen in the Black Hole, 'complaining a little of the hard usage of the English Honourable Company,' but assuring His Highness of their 'good intentions, notwithstanding what had happened, and begging'—for provisions. So run the minutes of the Bengal Council held on board the *Phoenix* schooner at Fulta on August 22, 1756.

To this broken band came Admiral Watson in December with a fleet and an army. It should be remembered that Admiral Watson, not Colonel Clive, commanded the expedition; although the Admiral proved his patriotism at a critical moment by waiving his rights, and so averted a deadlock between the sea and land forces. Within eight months he delivered Calcutta, and captured the strongholds higher up the river—Hugli city from the native power, Chandarnagar from the French—and turned the great sea-entrance to Bengal for once and for ever into a British highway. At the end of that half-year of hard fighting he died on August 16, 1757, in the flower of manhood and with honour at its height. They laid him among the ruins of St. John's churchyard, which he had wrested back from the destroyers. Yet even on his tomb, with its '*Exegit monumentum aere perennius*,' the reptiles of that age did not fear to spill their slaver. They had forged the Admiral's name to Clive's fictitious treaty, and found a confederate to aver that it was done with the dead hero's connivance and cowardly assent.

England meanwhile had won the water-gate of Bengal, and a practical nation does not too closely count the cost. But what those eight months of fighting meant may be learned from one fact. Soon after Watson's death his gallant comrade, Major Kilpatrick, was buried, in October, 1757. 'Of the 250 soldiers who came with him [Kilpatrick] in August, 1756,' writes the Admiral's surgeon, 'only five survived their commander, and these were now by repeated sickness emaciated to the greatest degree.'

A single episode, however, tells that heroic story better than any nouns of multitude. When they brought Admiral Watson to St. John's church-yard, they dug his grave near to a mound newly raised over a midshipman of his own flag-ship. 'Billy' Speke was the son of Captain Henry Speke of the *Kent*, which carried the Admiral's red pennant at her mizzen-top-mast. During the capture of the French settlement Chandarnagar, or Fort Orleans on the Hugli as it was called, the *Kent* received 138 cannon-shot through her side next the fort, her decks were swept with grape, her masts and rigging hacked to pieces, and within three hours 111 of her crew lay wounded or dead. Captain Speke and his son, a lad of sixteen years the doctor says, were struck at the same moment. The wounded Captain, seeing his boy's leg hanging only by the skin, remarked to the Admiral, 'Indeed, sir, this was a cruel shot to knock down both the father and the son.' 'Mr. Watson's heart was too full to make the least reply,' writes the surgeon, disjointed sentences from whose narrative may complete the tale.

After doing what he could for the father, Dr. Ives went to the son. But the lad would not allow him to touch the leg until the surgeon assured him 'upon my honour' that his father's wound had been dressed and promised well. 'Then,' replied the boy, 'pray, sir, look to and dress this poor man who is groaning so sadly beside me.' 'I told him that he already had been taken care of. He calmly observed, "Sir, I fear you must amputate above the joint." I replied, "My dear, I must!" Upon which he clasped both his hands together, and lifting his eyes in the most devout and fervent manner towards heaven, he offered up the following short but earnest petition: "Good God, do Thou enable me to behave worthy of my father's son." I then performed the operation above the joint of the knee; but during the whole time the intrepid youth never spake a word or uttered a groan that could be heard at a yard distance.'

Throughout the long torture of the amputation, the father lay stretched close to his son. 'But whatever were his [the father's] feelings, we discovered no other expressions of them than what the silent trickling tears declared, though the bare recollection of the scene, even at this distant time, is too painful for me.' Next morning both were taken, together with the rest of the wounded, to Calcutta: the father being lodged in a relative's house, the poor boy in the hospital under the doctor's own eye. After thirteen days of agony, aggravated by anxieties for his father, and apparently by Voices in fevered dreams whispering that his father was dead, the end came. 'The dear youth had been delirious,' continues the doctor, 'the evening preceding the day on which he died, and at two o'clock in the morning, in the utmost distress of mind, he sent me an incorrect note written by himself with a pencil, of which the following is an exact copy: "*If Mr. Ives will consider the disorder a son must be in when he is told he is dying and is yet in doubt whether his father is not in as good a state of health. If Mr. Ives is not too busy to honour this chitt* [short note], *which nothing but the greatest uneasiness could draw from me. The boy waits an answer.*"'

The incoherent appeal scrawled by a rushlight, and with almost the last flicker of the boyish brain amid the reeking night-fumes of the hospital, quickly brought the doctor to the bedside. 'He then began with me. "And is he dead?" "Who, my dear?" "My father, sir." "No, my love; nor is he in any danger, I assure you. He is almost well." "Thank God, then why did THEY tell me so? I am now satisfied and ready to die!" He begged my pardon for having (as he obligingly and tenderly expressed himself) disturbed me at so early an hour, and'—died.

He sleeps in brave company. Our Calcutta graveyards, indeed, are sown so thick with heroes as to leave small space for separate monuments. A cenotaph hard by was set up on twelve pillars in memory of a like number of officers who fell in a desperate conflict with the Rohillas in 1796. Inside there is a platform designed for some military trophy, never erected. Nor was there even a list of their names nor any epitaph until a hundred years later, when the Government in 1895 placed the present inscription. The brave little midshipman, 'Billy' Speke, lies not far from a tomb which thriftily commemorates two founders of our Indian Empire. A slab within its recess bears the name of the patriotic surgeon, Hamilton, who in 1715 asked as fee from an Emperor a grant of privileges to his countrymen. Another slab records in 1693 the death of Charnock, the originator of Calcutta. One sepulchre now suffices for the founder and the benefactor of the British capital of India.

It is difficult to say whether the founder or the benefactor fared worse at the hands of those whom they served. Of Surgeon William Hamilton, described in the Calcutta burial register by the honourable title of Physician, the tablet truly says that 'his memory ought to be dear to this nation.'

As a matter of fact, while he was curing the Delhi Emperor at the risk of his own life if the operation went wrong, and exhausting his credit with his august patient to obtain indulgences for the English Company, his Honourable Masters had, in a fit of parsimony on the other side of the globe, done away with his appointment, and ordered 'the discharge of Dr. Hamilton on his return from Court.'

From this ingratitude the Directors were spared partly by the fear of losing Hamilton's influence with the Emperor, and partly by Hamilton's death. 'Finding by the letters before us,' they wrote grudgingly in their Bengal despatch of January 1717, 'how successful he hath been in curing the Great Mogul, which very probably will help forward our negociations and get an easier grant of some of our requests, we now say that if Dr. Hamilton shall desire a continuance in our service, you readily consent to it, and let him see you are sensible of the benefit accruing to us, if you find he any hath, by his undertaking and accomplishing that cure.'

The noble doctor was saved from putting to the test these tardy good intentions. The Emperor, reluctant to part with the man who had given him back health, loaded him with gifts, among them 'models of all his surgical instruments in pure gold.' At length the Physician, said the Persian inscription on his original grave-stone, 'having made his name famous in the four quarters of the earth by the cure of the Emperor, the Asylum of the World, and with a thousand difficulties having obtained permission from the Imperial Court, which is the Refuge of the Universe, to return to his own country, by the Divine decree on the fourth of December, 1717, died in Calcutta, and is buried here.' The epitaph was evidently written, the grave-stone was perhaps paid for, by some grateful Moslem friend.

The story of the founder of Calcutta is even a more sorrowful one. Job Charnock went to India in 1655 or 1656, and got a five years' engagement under the Company. His Honourable Masters in England soon discovered his value, and retained him in their service by appointing him chief of the Patna Factory, probably in 1664. There he remained until 1680, married a Hindu wife, and adopted customs of the natives around him. The lady is said to have been a girl-widow of good caste, whom he rescued at the risk of his own life while she was being led out to her husband's funeral pyre. Cut off by her re-marriage from orthodox Hinduism, she appears to have joined one of the sects which in India mitigated the harshness of the caste system by holding out a fresh start to the unfortunate and the out-caste. After many wedded years Charnock cherished her memory by an anniversary sacrifice of a cock upon her tomb: an adaptation from the rites of the Five Saints of Behar, the province in which he had rescued and married her. In 1680 he was promoted to the more central charge of the Company's house of business near the modern Murshidabad, with the claim to succeed as chief of all the factories in Bengal at Hugli town.

To Charnock fell the perilous task of settling the position of the English towards the native powers. We had gone to India in 1600 as simple traders, and during three quarters of a century we trafficked as peaceably as we could under the protection of the Mughal Empire. But before 1680 the decay of that Empire had set in, and the Emperor could no longer shield our factories from the oppressions of his own provincial deputies. It was not so much the want of will on the part of the central Mughal Government to deal fairly with the foreigners who proved so profitable to its exchequer. It was the want of power. Gradually the English agents were forced to the conclusion that if they were to remain in India they must defend themselves. Charnock had struggled against the exactions and extortions of the native officials for thirty years. More than once he saw his masters' property despoiled. He himself was said to have suffered the indignity of the lash by command of a local ruler. In 1686 he slipped through the cordon of soldiers who had surrounded his factory near Murshidabad, and assumed charge of the Company's head-quarters in Bengal, at Hugli town. He stood forth as the champion of the new maxim, which then began to be adopted by our countrymen in India, that 'A fort is better than an ambassador.'

In converting this phrase into a reality, Charnock spent the remaining seven years of his hard and harassed life. Worn out by thirty years of unbroken labour in the tropics, he had already been once superseded from home in his claim to the chief charge of the Company's affairs in Bengal, and he was destined to again suffer the same injustice. By 1686, however, even his Honourable Masters in London realized that their only choice on the Hugli river lay between self-defence and flight. As the native governors, they wrote, have 'got the knack of trampling upon us, and extorting what they please of our estate from us by the besieging of our Factorys and stopping of our boats upon the Ganges, they will never forbear doing so till we have made them as sensible of our power as we have of our truth and justice.' They accordingly obtained leave from King James the Second to commence hostilities, and in 1686 sent out a force to be placed under Charnock's command in Bengal.

Their plan was to exact redress by capturing the Mughal ships, or failing that, to abandon their head-quarters in Hugli town, and seize and fortify a position near the mouth of the river, or at Chittagong further east along the Bay. The worthy Directors in London had a very vague idea as to where Chittagong really was, and it did not occur to them that their scheme would cut them off from the internal commerce of Bengal. Charnock at once saw that what the proposed new settlement might gain in safety it must lose in trade. The problem before him was to find a place secure from attack, yet commanding the traffic of the Ganges.

This problem he solved in spite of difficulties and discouragements such as no other founder of British rule in India has had to overcome. There is a reach of the Hugli river, twenty-seven miles below Hugli town and about eighty miles from the sea, where the stream scoops for itself a long deep pool—now the port of Calcutta. The place was early known to the Portuguese, whose galliasses from 1530 onwards anchored there, to transfer cargo to country craft, and so avoid the further dangers of the river which shallows above the pool.

On the arrival of the fleet from Goa each year, a bazaar of mat huts sprang up on the west bank of the river. On the departure of the Portuguese vessels, after transhipping their cargo, the mat huts were burned down, and the place returned to solitude until the return of the Goa fleet in the next season. In course of time some mean mud hovels, known as Sutanati Hat, literally 'Cotton Thread Mart,' struggled into existence on the eastern bank for the sale of the country-made yarns and cloths. Protection was given, during the better days of the Mughal Empire, by a petty fort on either side of the river below the pool, as a defence against water-pirates and land-marauders. But the poor mud hamlet of 'Cotton Mart' on the east bank appeared scarcely less insignificant than the bazaar of mat huts which was annually set up and burned down on the western edge of the channel.

It seemed as if nature had determined that the reach should be one of anchorage only, and no abiding-place for man. From the west bank stretched a country ravaged by great rivers during a third of the year, and open during the other two-thirds to the banditti of the most turbulent districts of southern Bengal. If the traders who flocked together to supply the Goa fleet had not burned down their mat huts, the raiders from the west would have promptly saved them the trouble.

The eastern side of the river appeared even more impracticable for human habitation. One or two families of Sets and Baisaks, indeed, settled at the Cotton Mart on the high east bank overlooking the river. But that bank sloped down behind into a swampy jungle, which at places came right to the river-edge. At others there was a strip of fairly raised ground between the river and the swamp, a strip nowhere then exceeding a mile in breadth. Behind it spread the vast agglomeration of brackish lagoons now known, within their curtailed limits, as the Salt Water Lakes—a pestilent region long given up to the tiger and the crocodile. By creeks through the narrow strip of high ground along the river bank, the fetid ooze from these fens swayed backward and forward with the rise and fall of the tide.

The truth is that an old channel of the Ganges, which took off eastwards from the Hugli a little below Cotton Mart Hamlet, had silted up during the three previous centuries. By 1686 it had dwindled into a line of shallow ponds, and no longer sufficed to draw off the mass of water from the brackish fens. A drowned land was thus formed, at that time stretching over a hundred square miles, shut off from its old exit southwards towards the sea, and poisoning with its stagnant slush the country around. Yet this very region of swamp rendered the Hugli bank at Cotton Mart unapproachable by troops from the east. Charnock saw that a European Power which dared the unhealthiness of the spot, and whose ships commanded the river, would, whatever it suffered from nature, be safe from the attack of man.

There is a story of how the old man landed at the place, and sat under a great tree pondering on its possibilities for a settlement. But the facts need no aid from legend. His Honourable Masters had sent him four hundred men, with orders to make war upon an empire that counted its armies by millions, and whose garrison in the outlying fort of Hugli alone numbered 3,300 horse and foot. He knew that half a century before, in 1632, the Mughal troops destroyed the Portuguese settlement at Hugli—a settlement far more powerful than the little company of Englishmen under his command—and carried off the whole Portuguese population as slaves a thousand miles inland. But he had small time for reflection. On October 28, 1686, a street fight between three of his soldiers and the market people in Hugli town ended in a general attack. Charnock beat off the native garrison, and after fruitless negotiation put the Company's goods and servants on board his ships, dropped down the river twenty-seven miles, and anchored in the long deep pool opposite Cotton Mart Hamlet.

During the four following months he made some sort of settlement on the high river bank, and even hoped for permission to build a fort. But in February, 1687, the Imperial forces began to press upon him from above. After a gallant fight he had again to take to his ships and seek shelter about seventy miles further down the river, near its mouth. There he tried to fortify himself at Hijili, which, although on the east bank, was protected to landward by a network of swamps and creeks. A high dyke now circles the region like the rampart of a Roman camp, and defends it to some extent from inundation. It was then but half rescued from the sea, 'having a great store of wild hogs, deer, wild buffaloes and tigers,' at places fertile, but so malarious that it passed into a Hindustani proverb.

In this weird land, where the Company's servants had stalked big game in happier days, Charnock and his four hundred sought refuge at the end of February, 1687. He seized a little fort, but the Nawab's army again closed upon him with 12,000 men. In three months Charnock buried two hundred of his soldiers, only one hundred remained fit to bear arms, many of them but living skeletons, almost all of them emaciated with fever and ague. Of forty officers, only himself and one lieutenant with four sergeants were alive and able for duty. Their principal ship sprang another great leak, and the end seemed to have come, when a vessel hove in sight from England with seventy fresh men on board.

Charnock, who had been the soul of the defence, now obtained honourable terms of capitulation. On June 11, 1687, he marched out the remnant of his men, gaunt and ragged, but with drums beating and colours flying. After trying another place, Ulabaria halfway up the river, for three months, he once more anchored in the long deep pool opposite Cotton Mart Hamlet. Here he again opened negotiations for leave to build a fort on the eastern bank, and meanwhile stoutly set to work with brick and lime on the river edge which was destined to become Calcutta.

For a year he laboured at the double task of buying a treaty from the Nawab, and erecting a factory in anticipation of it. The rugged veteran seems to have been quite unconscious that he was doing anything heroic. His Honourable Masters, indeed, so far from thanking him, marvelled at 'your insensible patience' under the oppressions of the native viceroy. Nor were they 'without great fear that your backwardness and hankering after your profitable, easy old habitations [at Hugli town], as the Israelites did after the onions and garlick of Egypt, may deprive us of the fruit of all our cost.' As to his magnificent defence of Hijili, 'it was not your wit or contrivance, but God Almighty's good providence, which hath always graciously superintended the affairs of the Company,' to which he owed his deliverance. So in 1688 they sent out a hot-headed sea-captain to supersede the old man, with a plan of campaign drawn up in a London counting-house.

Charnock had now tried four places on the

river: Hugli town, 100 miles from the sea; Ulabaria, literally 'the abode of owls,' halfway down; Hijili, near the mouth; and twice over the long pool at Cotton Mart, with its high eastern bank protected by swamps to the landward. With infinite labour and endurance of misery through the hot weather and the drenching rains of 1688, he hutted his fever-stricken followers, and began some poor defensive works. To him arrived on September 20, 1688, Captain Heath with a reproachful despatch from the Directors, and orders to load their goods once more on ship and to sail for Chittagong.

Charnock pleaded hard for his rising settlement. The despatch grudgingly provided that if he had already fortified some suitable place, their servants might stay there, 'since we can't now help it.' With the aid of this argument he managed to delay the catastrophe for seven weeks. But Captain Heath, although a skilful navigator, had not the eye of genius with which Charnock, and Clive after him, discerned the strength of the high eastern bank of the Calcutta pool alike for commerce and for war. After much wrangling and several sudden changes of mind, the impetuous sailor put Charnock with the Company's other servants and goods on board, and sailed away, leaving the factors at the inland stations, and even our envoys at the Nawab's Court, to their fate.

He had but a hazy notion as to whither he was going. His Honourable Masters distinctly ordered him to capture Chittagong. But their despatch from London shows that they fancied he would find that place somewhere 'up the great Ganges!' As a matter of fact, it lay on a little river far to the east, and was cut off from the inland Gangetic trade. During three months Heath prowled round the Bay of Bengal with the Company's whole Bengal establishment on board, sacked and burned a sea-coast town, looked in at Chittagong only to find it defended by 10,000 men, vainly offered his services to the Arrakan king, and after again abandoning an envoy, sought refuge in a rage at Madras. His overcrowded human cargoes had been dying of scurvy, and in February, 1689, as he himself writes, he gave 'orders for each ship to make the best of her way.'

At Madras, Charnock, with the other Bengal servants of the Company, abode in a sort of exile for fifteen weary months. But the indefatigable Nestor soon set to work to patch up the ruin which Heath had brought to the settlement in Bengal. After long negotiations, the refugees were allowed to return. It was a perilous step; even Charnock hesitated for a moment, and the sturdy Welsh chaplain Evans of the Bengal establishment preferred to remain at Madras for a season, to preach and trade in safety. At length, on Sunday, August 24, 1690, at noon, Charnock and his Council and factors, for the third time, anchored in the long pool of the Hugli river at Cotton Mart. They 'found the place,' says their Consultation Book under that date, 'in a deplorable condition, nothing being left for our present accommodation, and the rain falling day and night.' With a poor guard of thirty soldiers all told, they scrambled up the steep mud-bank which was thenceforward, without a break, to grow into the British capital of India.

If Charnock had given a thought to his ease he would have sailed on to Hugli town, and settled there under the assurances of the now friendly viceroy. But he knew the value of such assurances, which, although they might hold good long enough for individuals to make a fortune, formed no permanent guarantee to the Company. He turned a deaf ear alike to native persuasions and the clamours of his own countrymen, who longed for their houses and gardens in Hugli town, and for the private trade there which alone rendered Indian service bearable. He had had enough of 'fenceless factories,' and, in spite of shattered health, he resolved to bequeath to his masters a stronghold that should be better than an ambassador, even if he perished in the attempt. He perished: but not until, by two more years of endurance, he had founded Calcutta.

They were two miserable years. The buildings which he set up in 1688 with so much labour and peril had been plundered and burnt. Three ruined mud hovels alone remained on the high river-bank. Through the pitiless rains of 1690 he struggled sternly on, although the declaration of war by England against the French, whose settlement lay twenty-four miles higher up the river, seemed to make his efforts the mere obstinacy of a dotard. In the scorching summer of 1691 an official despatch describes him and his desponding Council as still dwelling in 'only tents, hutts, and boats.' It is not surprising that he sent home 'an incomplete cargo' that year, for which the Company's governor amid the plenty of Madras soundly rated him.

His own followers still sighed for their 'profitable, easy old habitations' at Hugli town, and saw with chagrin a nest of interlopers flock thither under the protection of the native ruler and monopolize their private trade. Even as late as 1693, when Chaplain Evans returned from his money-making and preaching in Madras, it was not with the struggling settlement at Calcutta but with the interlopers at Hugli that the astute Welshman threw in his lot. This active parson lived to take his wealth home to England, was rapidly preferred to the see of Bangor, and being translated thence to Armagh, the premier bishopric of Ireland, died at a ripe age in the odour of sanctity.

Yet in spite of everything Calcutta grew. When once fortified, its position secured it on three sides from attack. Its deep harbour attracted the trade from the Dutch and French settlements on the shallow reaches higher up the river, and the native merchants began to crowd to a place where they felt safe. It was perceived that a few armed ships in the Calcutta pool could cut off the upper settlements from the sea. But the fever-haunted swamps which stretched behind the high river-bank exacted a terrible price for its prosperity. The name of Calcutta, taken from a neighbouring Hindu shrine, was identified by our mariners with Golgotha—the place of skulls. Within a decade after Charnock finally landed on the deserted river-bank in 1690, it had become a busy native mart with 1250 European inhabitants, of whom 450 were buried between the months of August and January in one year. The miseries of the fever-stricken band throughout 1690 and 1691 are not to be told in words.

By the middle of 1692 they had made firm their footing. Indeed, the official records complain that Charnock secured a larger investment for the Company in that year than he had funds to pay for. The battle was won, but Charnock was not to enjoy the victory. His last months were embittered by a subordinate who taunted him with the new Company about to be formed in England, and of which 'he and not Charnock would be the chief in Bengal.' A terror of getting enmeshed within the distant jurisdiction of the Madras court paralyzed his action and haunted his bedimmed mind. The shadows of coming night settled heavily on the worn-out man. He grew moody and savage. The government slipped from him into unworthy hands. His closing days were unlovely and unloved. On January 10, 1693, they buried him in a grim enclosure, destined in the next century to become the site of the Old Cathedral of Calcutta.

What little the English world knew of him was for long made up of stories of his last morose years, told by interlopers who hated him, and by an unworthy successor who failed to discern what he had achieved. Even Orme, the most careful of Indian historians, misled by the old style date on his tomb, gives a wrong year for his death—an error followed, I believe, by all writers down to 1888. Charnock now stands forth in the manuscript records as a block of rough hewn British manhood. Not a beautiful personage perhaps, for the founders of England's greatness in India were not such as wear soft raiment and dwell in kings' houses; but a man who had a great and hard task to do, and who did it—did it with small thought of self, and with a resolute courage which no danger could daunt nor any difficulties turn aside.

The masters who treated him so grudgingly knew his worth. He was even in his lifetime our 'honest Mr. Charnock'; no 'prowler for himself beyond what was just and modest.' But the inscription on his tomb, written, let us hope, by Chaplain Evans, bishop and merchant, mutely appeals to a higher verdict than man's. He sleeps '*in spe beatae resurrectionis ad Christi iudicis adventum*'—an exile '*qui postquam in solo non suo peregrinatus esset diu, reversus est domum suae aeternitatis.*' He abides in the hope of a joyful resurrection at the coming of Christ the Judge: a wanderer who after long travel in a far country has returned to his eternal home. Perhaps his truest epitaph is a chance line in a despatch from the Directors a year after his death—'Always a faithful Man to the Company.'

There he rests, CONDITOR URBIS, in the heart of the vast hot city, with nigh a million human beings surging around. On the one side tower the buildings of the great Calcutta newspaper, with the nightly whir of its steam-press. On the other stands the Old Cathedral of St. John, with the twitter of birds from its eaves at sunrise, and the moving shadow of its steeple and chime of hours throughout the glaring day. Tropical trees in their unchanging greenness keep watch over all. His tomb is the oldest piece of masonry above ground in Calcutta. The graves of his contemporaries have long been covered by accretions of soil and silt. The generations of dead Englishmen who beat out their hard lives in Bengal through the seventeenth century are sunk deep below the surface. They lie as remote from modern ken as the tropical insect life that buzzed and fluttered in the jungles which now form the peat-beds twenty feet under Calcutta.

Thirty of their head-stones, dug up during excavations or rescued from church repairs, were formed into a paved terrace around Chárnock's mausoleum. For Surgeon Hamilton's, a place was found within it. The finely raised letters on the hard slabs give dates from 1693 to 1766. The instinctive piety of later Englishmen has thus made the founder's tomb the centre of a Campo Santo for the men who did England's work in Bengal, and died, and were traduced or forgotten.

The very ground on which they struggled and suffered has disappeared. The old foundations of forts, factories, council-chambers, and churches lie buried one under the other—silently obliterated by successive layers of silt. Even the site of the Black Hole was unknown until revealed by recent excavations. Calcutta rises phoenix-like above her ruins, with the Hugli river as her one unchanging landmark, recalling a yet more august scene of decay and new birth:

> Ne ought save Tyber hastning to her fall
> Remaines of all: O world's inconstancie!
>   That which is firme doth flit and fall away,
>   That which is flitting doth abide and stay.

Envy and evil-speaking are now so happily abated in India, and backbiting, like a good Christian's charity, is so scrupulously done in secret, that a man has only to be sure of himself to live unperturbed by the rancour of rivals or the jealousy of friends. Defamation itself takes refuge in negatives. But from the calumnies of cliques these dead men had no outside appeal. They could not pay back detraction with contempt. An iron-hooped orbit of officialism hemmed in their only known sphere of public life. Until India passed to the Crown in 1858, England troubled herself little about Indian administration, save once in twenty years at the successive wrangles over the Company's charter. For a full century after Charnock founded Calcutta, the power of the Press was unknown in Bengal.

Nor, indeed, did that power at first prove for good. The earliest Calcutta newspaper, *Hicky's Bengal Gazette* (1780), was proscribed, not unjustly, within its first ten months, after which no copy might pass through the Post Office. Its later numbers, nauseous mixtures of dullness and indecency, were written and edited in jail. During fifty years its successors uttered their feeble voices in peril of deportation and under menace of the censor's rod. Scurrility and servility, indeed, long seemed the only two notes known to Calcutta journalism. Who could have foreseen that those cat-callings of bugle-boys, practising their prentice windpipes in some out-of-the-way angle of the ramparts, were destined to grow into clear trumpet notes which should arouse sleeping camps to great constitutional struggles, and sound the charge of political parties in battle?

In place of the free praise or blame of public opinion, these dead men might obtain an entry in *The Bengal Obituary*, if their friends paid for a tombstone. That compilation was printed in 1848 by a worthy firm of Calcutta undertakers who, with a view to trade, traced the origin of monuments to 'the Universal Deluge, when the Rainbow was made or selected as a standing token.' It piously encouraged the public to 'proper sepulture' by the argument of 'the Resurrection of the Body.' Its inscriptions from the old Calcutta burial-grounds and the rural graveyards of Northern India, dating with a few exceptions from 1768 onwards, form the sole memorial of many a brave soldier and manful ruler of districts.

We forget the harsh judgments passed on our predecessors in India while turning over these pious flatteries from their tombs. Perhaps the truth lies between the two legends. We learn, at any rate, that amid the unbeautiful life of Calcutta a century and a half ago, mothers sorrowed for little children in the same tender words of Scripture which they still use, that fair wives died young, and that men went to their graves convoyed by troops of friends. What a record here, too, of hopes shattered, ambitions wrecked, and promise unfulfilled! The collapse of the banking houses in Calcutta, with their failure for seventeen millions sterling between 1830 and 1834, involved in one gigantic ruin the military and civilian families of Bengal. Some of the old names survive in the two great Services, but many went down in the flood, or were cast up as jetsam in subordinate branches of public employ. Very few, like the Thackerays, still flourish numerously not only in their own name but through branching female lines. The undertaker's volume preserves the epitaphs of the multitude that have disappeared.

The noble Service which formed the governing body in India has, in one respect, suffered most. Our early wars still move before us in the living pages of Orme. The Bengal army, the Madras army, the Company's artillery and navy has each its separate historian; the soldier politicals have an honourable literature of their own. The Indian Civil Service has found no annalist. If an Indian administrator happened to belong to some close evangelical borough at Madras or Serampur, he received the doubtful honours of an 'improving' biography. Otherwise he passed to his grave unknown, unless some one had something to say against him. Till Bosworth Smith's *Life of Lord Lawrence* awakened by its manly narrative the interest of England, the world heard little good of Indian civilians except in sectarian memoirs, or in the more disastrous panegyrics of filial piety.

For this, the two principles of the old Civil Service, patronage and seniority, were in part to blame. All seniority services are jealous of exceptional success. In the army, the principle of seniority is tempered by the battle-field and the brevet. The old Bengal Civil Service had no such sanctions for short-cuts to greatness, and it regarded brilliancy of any sort with a coldly distrustful eye. Its *esprit de corps* was the *esprit de corps* of aunts, sisters, and cousins; a family feeling which bound with feminine withes many a strong man's hands, but which had small sympathy for talent without relatives, and made no defence for it if it fell.

The only amends that these poor dead civilians could offer to their Service for exceptional ability was an early death. It was an apology at once pathetic and complete. Yet even the name of Augustus Clevland, the *dulce decus* of the old Bengal Civil Service, has been misspelt during a century; and the date of Vans Agnew's burial on the summit of a captured citadel remained incomplete, when I last read his Calcutta cathedral tablet, as '184–.' The neglect of our countrymen's graves in India long formed a reproach to the British name. Perhaps it still does. If the early English in Calcutta stoned their prophets, their successors grudged a little quicklime to whiten their tombs.

In the same graveyard in which Francis laid his wrathful colleagues to rest, a tapering column with a spiral fluting round it commemorates a poet's early love. The faint lettering on its tablet bears the name of Rose Aylmer, whose beauty and sweetness for a time brought calm to Landor's troubled spirit. After his mishap at Oxford, and having quitted his father's house as he vowed 'for ever,' Landor sought retirement on the Welsh coast in 1796. There he found kindness from Lord Aylmer's family, and chiefly from the gifted daughter Rose.

He was about twenty-one: she barely seventeen. The most gracefully tender of his poems tell the old tale; the joyous awakening of young hearts; the rambles by wood and shore; his briar-torn hand which she bound up; the tune she softly sang— 'How close I bent I quite forget, I only know I hear it yet.' It was a book which Rose lent him that struck the first true outflash of Landor's genius in *Gebir*. 'Sold for a shilling, it has miraculous beauties,' wrote Southey of that almost forgotten work. 'I would go a hundred miles to see the anonymous author.' Then came the warning voice, 'Whispering happy as thou art, Happiness and thou must part.' Lady Aylmer married a second time, and Rose was sent out to her aunt, Lady Russell, in Calcutta. A pathetic verse of Landor hints that she went not of her own choice.

Whatever her secret sorrow, she had not to bear it long. The *Calcutta Gazette* of the first week of March, 1800, records her death—aged twenty, says the tombstone. 'Her noble name she never changed,' wrote Landor, 'Nor was her nobler heart estranged.' The news fell on him midway in his erratic youth. For days and nights her image never left his brain. During hours of sleeplessness he wrote the elegy which enshrines in a casket of pearl the name of Rose Aylmer as long as maiden hearts shall ache and the English language endure:

Ah what avails the sceptred race?
  Ah what the form divine?
What every virtue, every grace?
  Rose Aylmer, all were thine.
Rose Aylmer, whom these wakeful eyes
  May weep but never see,
A night of memories and of sighs
  I consecrate to thee.

How various the fates which these Calcutta graveyards chronicle! Not far from Rose Aylmer's tapering column, George Foley, the brilliant young civilian sent in 1786 against the recalcitrant Rajas and 'armed multitude' of the west, lies with but a name and date, and a pitiful little epitaph in half-caste French: 'Ce monument est construit par une Amie.' The amaranth of Love Lies Bleeding blooms ever amid our deserts of death. Its very name of amaranth springs from the same root as the Indian word for Immortality.

In the Calcutta cemeteries, as in our Station

graveyards throughout Bengal, the tiny graves rise close. The price of the British rule in India has always been paid in the lives of little children. To many of the early fathers of Calcutta the curse on the rebuilder of Jericho came bitterly home: 'He shall lay the foundation thereof in his first-born, and in his youngest son shall he set up the gates of it.' Certain families seem, indeed, to have been specially singled out for this sorrow. In the same South Park Street graveyard, each generation of the Bayleys during the first half of the century laid a child; one of them burying two infant sons within two years.

Young or old, whether torn from the sobbing mother's breast, or calmly garnered in the ripeness of years, defacing time has dealt impartially with their tombs. The places are very desolate. Some of the monuments are in ruins, some coarsely patched up, others have been levelled with the ground. From many the inscription slabs have fallen out, and the names and dates can only be gathered from *The Bengal Obituary*. That pathetically stolid jumble now forms the best record of a century of tenderness and greatness and grief.

CHAPTER II

THACKERAY'S GRANDFATHER IN BENGAL

FASHIONABLE Park Street appears in the map of Calcutta for 1794 as Burial Ground Road. But Sir Elijah Impey, when Chief Justice, had located himself with magnificence on its southern edge, near the present Loretto Convent, and turned the adjacent waste into a deer-park. Other stately mansions sprang up around his enclosure. A later Chief Justice, Sir Henry Russell, to whose wife poor Rose Aylmer was sent about 1798, built the palace which gave its name to Russell Street on the west of Sir Elijah's pleasure-grounds. Camac Street was cut out of their eastern margin, and houses gradually filled up the intervening space. Impey's old deer-park thus grew into the crowded Mayfair of Calcutta, and the route along its northern side to the graveyards was euphemized from Burial Ground Road into Park Street. 'All funeral processions,' says an early Calcutta writer, 'are concealed as much as possible from the sight of the ladies, that the vivacity of their tempers may not be wounded.'

On September 13, 1815, a train of merchants, soldiers, and dignitaries defiled along that road behind the coffin of a civilian struck down midway in his career. I wonder if the chief mourner was a pale-faced little boy of four, who has come to be known in all English-speaking lands as the great-hearted satirist of our age, and the prime master of our full-grown English tongue? For it was the father of William Makepeace Thackeray whom Calcutta was escorting to his grave.

The year 1815 had been a death-dealing one to the Thackerays in Bengal. It opened with the news that the younger brother of the just deceased Richmond Thackeray was fallen in a desperate fight in Nepal. On August 14 Richmond headed the funeral procession of his cousin Henry to the military burial-ground in the southern suburb of Calcutta. And now within a month, on September 13, Richmond was himself carried forth for burial.

The Thackerays formed a typical family of the Bengal Civil Service in the days of John Company.

They threw out branches into the sister services, military and medical, and by a network of intermarriages created for themselves a ruling connexion both in India and in the Court of Directors at home. The first Thackeray in India went as a covenanted civilian in 1766, and four of his sons, with at least fourteen of his descendants and collaterals, have been traced in the same profession. While wandering over the three Presidencies, I noted down some of their many appearances in the old manuscript records, from the Malabar coast on the extreme south-west to the Sylhet valley in the far north-east of India. No published account exists of them; but I have been allowed to make use of a private Family Book of the Thackerays, compiled chiefly by an aunt of the novelist. The two sets of materials, when brought together from the Indian archives and the domestic papers, furnish a curious picture of one of those powerful and compact, but now almost extinct, family corporations which did so much to build up British rule in the East.

The Thackwas, Thackwras, or Thackerays, emerge in 1336 as holding thirty acres and a dwelling-house of the Abbot of St. Mary of Fountains. During the reign of James the First a branch of them took root at Hampsthwaite, a village in the West Riding of Yorkshire. There, from about 1600 to 1804 when the last of this line died childless, they dwelt as small owners, living in a manly way on the fringe of the moorland. From that modest home, in January, 1706, a boy of twelve years started southwards to be admitted as a King's Scholar at Eton, and by due stages to become a Fellow of King's College, Cambridge, an Eton master, Head-master of Harrow, Chaplain to the Prince of Wales, and Archdeacon of Surrey. He got his scholarship at King's College in 1711, exactly one hundred years before the birth of his great-grandson the novelist.

The prosperous ecclesiastic married in 1729 a daughter of John Woodward, Lord of the Manor of Butler's Marston, Warwickshire, and during the next twenty years had sixteen children. Indeed he accepted the Harrow head-mastership in 1746, on the birth of the fourteenth, chiefly with a view to getting his sons educated. Harrow School, although far on in its second century, had declined, under 'a drunken, disorderly, idle' head-master, to thirty-three boys, a number which increased to 130 during the vigorous rule of Dr. Thomas Thackeray. He died in 1760.

The heavily weighted widow thankfully accepted a Writership in the East India Company's service for her sixteenth and youngest child, William Makepeace, born in 1749. These two names formed a favourite combination among several branches of the Thackerays; derived, it is said, from a member of the family burned for his faith in the days of Queen Mary. William Makepeace Thackeray, grandfather of the novelist, was placed at the age of fourteen with a 'Writing-Master' at Bromley-by-Bow, to learn book-keeping—at that time essential for entering the Company's service. In August, 1765, his preceptor certified his capacity to the Court of Directors in somewhat guarded terms.

He 'has been under my care and instruction since midsummer, 1764,' wrote this worthy, 'has gone through a regular set of merchants' accounts and the practical rules of arithmetic, and I believe he understands what he has learned as well as most young gentlemen of his age and experience.' Accordingly in February, 1766, the lad sailed by the

Lord Camden for Calcutta, with a family Bible which his mother had used for fifty-three years, and which she gave him as her parting gift. The book has survived the many generations of Thackerays since passed away.

By the same ship sailed another youthful Writer, the son of Lord Sandwich and the celebrated Miss Ray. The poor boy died on his voyage out. A third was George Grand, the predestined husband of the fair daughter of the Capitaine du Port at Chandarnagar, whose seduction cost Sir Philip Francis fifty thousand rupees in 1779, and who ended her chequered career in 1835 as Princesse de Talleyrand. I found myself on board the *Lord Camden*, wrote Mr. Grand in his Narrative published at the Cape of Good Hope in 1814, 'accommodated with eleven Writers, each with a standing bed in the great cabin, not one of which gentlemen, excepting Mr. John Makepeace Thackeray of Hadley, is now (1802) living.' The 'John' is one of Mr. Grand's slips of memory.

The shipload of young civilians arrived in stirring times. The previous year, 1765, had brought the grant of Bengal from the Mughal Emperor to the East India Company, followed by Clive's despairing effort, as he said, 'to cleanse the Augean stable' of Anglo-Indian abuses. The elder civilians were banded against the Governor's attack on their private trade, while the English officers of the army formed a mutinous league against his military retrenchments. 'The office of Governor has been hunted down,' wrote Clive. But the victor of Plassey kept his Bengal hounds at bay, by bringing up four councillors from Madras, and by filling his secretariat with youths fresh from England.

Into this wild arena young Thackeray was dropped, with his mother's Bible in his trunk. His 'arrival as Writer' is dated in the Company's books, June 20, 1766, his seventeenth birthday, although the *Lord Camden* did not actually reach Calcutta till some weeks later. Placed with three others of his shipmates in the Secretary's office, he attracted the notice of his superiors, and was next year promoted to be assistant treasurer or 'cash-keeper' under the new Governor, Verelst. In the Company's pay-sheet for 1767 he draws Rs. 1158 or £145 per annum, while most of the other Writers only receive £80. Except during a brief appointment in the Calcutta Court, his first five years were passed in the financial and correspondence departments of the Government. Mr. Cartier, who succeeded to the governorship of Bengal in 1769, also employed him under his own eye. The first use that Thackeray made of his promotion was to relieve his widowed mother of the charge of two of his sisters. On their arrival in Calcutta the Governor behaved with fatherly kindness to the youthful group. It was at his house that the elder sister met her future husband. In the family records Thackeray appears at this time as 'Secretary to Mr. Cartier'; personal assistant would more correctly describe his position.

That position gave him a thorough insight into the mechanism of the Government. Clive had left behind a dual system, under which the actual administration remained apart from the superior control. The actual administration continued in the hands of the old native officials who collected the revenue. The superior control was exercised by a handful of Englishmen who could do little more than see the revenue duly forwarded to head-quarters, and invest it in calicoes or other country products for the yearly shipment home. Their business was not to dispense justice to the people, but to provide dividends for Leadenhall Street. Their official grades as Factors, Junior Merchants, Senior Merchants, Store-keepers and Export Warehouse-keepers, expressed their real duties. The profits on the Annual Investment still formed the touchstone of merit. Even in 1772 Warren Hastings was chosen for the Bengal governorship by reason of his good management of the warehouses at Madras.

In conducting the Company's commerce, its servants also did business on their own account. Their nominal salaries scarcely yielded a subsistence. These meagre stipends, which they looked on as retainers rather than as pay, they augmented sometimes a hundredfold by private trade and by presents from natives. Clive, under orders from the Court of Directors, forbad in 1765 the acceptance of presents over Rs. 4,000, and tried to restrict the private trade. During Thackeray's five years in Calcutta, 1766 to 1771, the taking of large presents began to be discreditable. But the

Court of Directors failed to enforce their prohibition of private commerce. Indeed a general meeting of the Company compelled them to reconsider their decision, and their repeated orders led to a series of compromises with a view to the regulation rather than to the abolition of their Bengal servants' trade.

The truth is, that the old system of nominal salaries supplemented by private trade had advantages which the general body of the Company was unwilling to forego. It enabled it to do its business with an appearance of economy highly appreciated by the shareholders. The experience acquired in private trade, it was also argued, made the Company's servants keener merchants and better agents for its Investment than they could become by any other training. During Thackeray's whole residence in Bengal the officials continued, without social disapproval or self-reproach, to do business on their own account. Sea-captains and super-cargoes in like manner grew rich by carrying private freight. Generals and regimental officers retired with fortunes made from the supply of clothing or commissariat to the troops.

This system, with its show of low salaries in the ledgers at Leadenhall Street, opened a wide door to abuses. Honourable men acted up to the standard of public honour in their time; dishonourable men fell below it. Whatever success Thackeray had in his early ventures, he conducted them under the eye of the Governor, apparently from the Governor's own house, and certainly in such a spirit as to retain the confidence and esteem of his master.

After five years of training at the centre of government, he was appointed to a more independent position in the interior. The Governor, Mr. Cartier, had spent his whole inland service at Dacca, except when he volunteered as an ensign with Clive's army in 1757 after the Black Hole. He knew the advantages of the place for private trade, and he determined to give to his young favourite the same opportunity of making a fortune as he himself had enjoyed. In 1771 he accordingly appointed Thackeray to be Factor and Fourth in Council at Dacca. The brother and two sisters put themselves and their belongings into large country boats, and wended their way eastwards across the delta of the Ganges. The journey was a slow one amid tropical swamps and vast jungles, in which the roar of the tiger could be heard through the night, and his foot-prints seen at his drinking-places in the morning. After days of rowing, and poling, and towing from the banks, they emerged on the confluence of waters over which Dacca reigned as a queen.

That great city formed the Mughal capital of Bengal in the seventeenth century. Shorn somewhat of its splendour by the removal of the Court to Murshidabad in 1704, it remained in 1771 the seat of a wealthy local nobility and the Company's head-quarters in Eastern Bengal. Its situation at the meeting of the deltas formed by the Ganges, the Brahmaputra, and the Meghna gave it the command of an inexhaustible commerce. A network of rivers brought down to its landing-stairs the products of the east, north, and west. Further south, the united waters spread out into an inland sea gradually opening upon the Bay of Bengal. The approach to Dacca, with its towers, palaces, temples and minarets, still unspoiled by time, formed in the last century a sight never to be forgotten.

The Thackeray party consisted of the brother

aged twenty-two, sister Henrietta aged twenty-five, and sister Jane aged thirty-two. Henrietta was strikingly handsome; the elder sister, although not a beauty, was a kind, unaffected woman, of whom her mother predicted, 'If there's a sensible man in India, he will find out Jane.' One of the most sensible had already found her out while on a visit to Governor Cartier in Calcutta, and was waiting at Dacca to welcome her.

Among his eager, fortune-seeking countrymen of the last century in Bengal, Major James Rennell stands forth as an unique figure—a calm, disinterested man of science. Born in 1742, and having at the age of five lost his father, an artillery captain, in the campaign of the Pays Bas, James Rennell was educated by the kindness of relatives, and entered the navy at fourteen. Fortunate in quickly seeing service, he still more distinguished himself by a habit of drawing plans of whatever action his ship was engaged in and of the ports which she visited. When the peace of Paris in 1763 seemed to end his chances in the British navy, he entered the East India Company's fleet. In the following year, 1764, he received an ensign's commission in the Bengal Engineers from Governor Vansittart, and was appointed surveyor of the Company's dominions in Bengal.

In that position he remained, without seeking promotion or concerning himself in money-making, throughout his thirteen years of Indian service. Indifferent to the vanities of social life, he kept a staff of draughtsmen in Calcutta, but buried himself in the recesses of Eastern Bengal to be near the centre of his work. Year after year he studied the great river-systems in which he discovered the key to the geography of the country. He watched their behaviour in the mighty floods of each rainy season, measured the new silt-islands which they deposited, and mapped out their altered courses in the dry weather, until he wrested from them their secrets as land-makers and land-destroyers, at once the waterways, the soil-carriers, and the race-dividers of Bengal.

On his labours our knowledge of the country rests. After his return to England in 1777 they won for him the highest rank among men of science. Still refusing offers of advancement, he quietly went on with his work until extreme old age, content, in the words of the President of the Royal Geographical Society, to be 'the leading geographer in England, if not in Europe, for a period of fifty years.' Rennell now divides his scientific supremacy with D'Anville of France and Ritter of Germany, but enjoys an undisputed pre-eminence for many-sidedness gained by practical work as a sailor, explorer, and surveyor on land and on sea.

His researches extended over the whole world and throughout all time, from 'The Geography of Herodotus,' 'The Retreat of the Ten Thousand,' St. Paul's shipwreck, and the topography of Babylon and Troy, to the Delta of the Ganges, the mountains of the Himalaya, the Gulf stream and Arctic currents, the Niger valley and Central Africa. It was he who worked out the geographical interpretation of Mungo Park's travels. All the honours of science, from the Copley Gold Medal of the Royal Society to Baron Walckenaer's magnificent *éloge* before the French Academy, Rennell reaped. For other distinctions he cared nothing. He died in 1830 at the age of eighty-seven, and lies buried in Westminster Abbey. 'Gentle, courteous, and simple minded,' writes Sir Clements Markham, 'he was the type of a perfect English gentleman.'

This beautiful-souled man of science soon became the avowed suitor of Jane Thackeray. The year of her arrival with her brother and sister in Dacca, however, nearly proved to be the year of his death. The task of surveying Bengal had to be carried out amid dangers from river-pirates, herds of trampling elephants, and roaming hosts of banditti, the fierce remnants of the native armies. On one occasion Rennell saved himself from the spring of a leopard only by thrusting a bayonet down its throat.

In 1766, five years before he met Jane Thackeray, he had been literally cut to pieces by a band of marauders, 800 strong. Having routed them in a pitched battle, he came unexpectedly upon them again the next morning with an escort too weak for defence. One sabre-stroke 'cut his right shoulder-blade through, and laid him open for nearly a foot down the back, cutting through or wounding several of the ribs.' A second slashed his left elbow, a third pierced the arm, a fourth came down on his hand depriving him for ever of the use of a forefinger, besides lesser thrusts and hacks. In this mangled state he had to be rowed three hundred miles in a boat to the nearest surgeon at Dacca, with such cataplasms of leaves and onions as the anxious affection of his native servants could devise for his wounds. After hanging for months between life and death, he recovered, to find himself promoted by Lord Clive to be Captain of Engineers and Surveyor-General of Bengal, at the age of twenty-four.

The long illness saved Rennell from a scarcely less serious danger. For while he was slowly alternating between fits of delirium and prostration, the officers of the army conspired against Clive's retrenchments. Careless about money himself, and indeed exceptionally well provided for by a salary amounting with allowances to £1,000 a year, Rennell felt deeply for his less fortunate comrades. His dying condition alone prevented him from being taken into their mutinous league. 'It was indeed,' he wrote, 'a lucky circumstance for me; for no doubt I should have been carried away with the stream, and should have entered into an association which has been attended with disgrace to all those concerned in it.' Though the retrenchments bore lightly upon his large pay, merely reducing it by £274 per annum, he did not hesitate to express his opinion as to the wrong inflicted on his brethren-in-arms. His letters home enable us to understand how the transaction appeared to one of the few Englishmen at that time in Bengal who was himself indifferent to fortune.

'In this affair,' Rennell wrote, 'we discover the generosity of the Company to a set of men who have conquered a territory equal in extent to the kingdom of France, and this in a climate that proves so prejudicial to European constitutions that scarce one out of seventy men returns to his native country. There is a passage in Rollin's *Ancient History* relating to the Carthaginians disbanding their mercenary troops after those troops had preserved the State from ruin, and the reflection on it perfectly suits the East India Company. "There," says Rollin, "you discover the genius of a State composed of merchants who make a traffic out of their fellow-creatures."'

In 1771, the year of the Thackerays' arrival at Dacca, Rennell had again to disperse a wolfish army of marauders who were levying contributions throughout Eastern Bengal. In fifteen days he marched his force 320 miles across difficult country under a blazing sun, scattered the enemy without a blow, and returned to Dacca completely successful, but with 'another violent attack of fever,' says Sir Clements Markham, 'which nearly carried him off.' His slow convalescence knit more closely the tie between him and Jane Thackeray. In the autumn they became engaged, and next year the family party went on a visit to Mr. Cartier in Calcutta. Jane was married from Mr. Cartier's house to Major Rennell on October 15, 1772.

Henrietta Thackeray, as became a beauty, made a more brilliant match. The Chief of the Council of Dacca was the head of the Company's affairs in Eastern Bengal. Mr. Cartier himself had held the post for about five years, and secured a fortune in it, before taking the higher flight which ended in the governorship of Bengal. In 1771 the Thackerays found the Chiefship filled by Mr. James Harris, who, like Mr. Cartier, had passed his whole inland service at Dacca and realized a fortune. Coming to India as a Writer in 1758, Mr. Harris was in 1771 well enough off to contemplate retirement. As Thackeray's superior officer he would see much of the young ladies, and no doubt played the part of host to the brother and sisters until they installed themselves in a house of their own at Dacca. He became attached to the charming Henrietta, and shortly after the return of Major and Mrs. Rennell to that station in the autumn of 1772, the marriage took place from Jane's new wedded home.

Mr. Harris retired from the service, and sailed with his bride on January 7, 1773, by the *Prince of Wales* for England. The same ship carried the generous friend of the family, Mr. Cartier, who handed over the governorship of Bengal to Warren Hastings in the previous April, but had remained on for ten months in Calcutta to settle his affairs. The ex-Governor was thus able to marry one of the Thackeray sisters from his house, and to form a pleasant Dacca party with the other sister and her husband on their voyage home.

James Harris seems to have been a man of the minor nabob type, common among retired Anglo-Indians of his time. He bought a country seat near Chelmsford and a town house in Great Ormonde Street, then a fashionable locality; drove four-in-hand, and lived in a style which left his fortune much diminished at his death. His widow, Henrietta Thackeray, was somewhat abruptly awakened to the fact on her sending the executor a list of twenty-five friends to whom she wished to present mourning rings. He shrewdly remarked that she had better keep the money for her children. Enough remained to enable her to settle comfortably at Hadley, near her brother William Makepeace after his retirement from Bengal. Of her descendants two have left an honourable record at Balliol College, several distinguished themselves in the army or at the bar, at least one went to India.

While Thackeray thus prosperously settled his sisters in marriage he was also prospering himself. His nominal salary, as fourth in the Dacca Council, appears on the Company's pay-sheet for 1771 as only Rs. 495, or say £62 per annum—about half his allowances during previous years under Governor Cartier in Calcutta. But whatever restrictions were placed on the personal dealings of the Chief of the

Council, who drew a compensating grant, the junior members had the privilege of private trade. They could not have bought their daily food and kept a roof over their heads without it. In making the Annual Investment for the Company they made investments for themselves.

The disorganized state of inland commerce also led the Government to allow its servants to contract for many of its local requirements. It did so on the ground that they were often the only trustworthy purveyors whom it could find to deal with in the rural districts. They took contracts for grain for the army, building materials for forts, transport animals and boats for the conveyance of troops and treasure. Almost every one of them gave his name or protection to some native merchant and received a share of the profits.

Under the old system, against which the Court of Directors inveighed, the Company's servants claimed exemption from the transit duties levied on all other merchandise. This unfair privilege was abolished by Lord Clive's reforms, and the Company's servants had to conduct their private dealings subject to well-understood restrictions. To reconcile the practice permitted in India with the letter of the instructions from home, it became common for them to trade under the name of a native partner. The Court of Directors, while continuing to protest, knew that they could only put a stop to such transactions by a general rise in salaries from which they still shrank. There had always been a wide space between orders issued on this side of the globe and their execution on the other. More than once that interval saved our position in India. Charnock, as we saw, founded Calcutta in the teeth of Leadenhall Street.

Thackeray soon had an opportunity of still further increasing his fortune. The Dual Government left behind by Clive had visibly broken down, and in 1772 the Company resolved to stand forth as the sole responsible Government in Bengal. Under its orders Warren Hastings, the new Governor-General, appointed a British 'Collector' or Chief for the administration of each circle or District. Thackeray was selected as the first 'Collector' of the dangerous frontier province of Sylhet. In this great outlying angle of North-eastern Bengal new branches of commerce opened to him. Sylhet, with its virgin forests and mineral wealth, supplied the materials for the new fortress and city of Calcutta, several hundred miles off at the other end of the great river highway. The Hon. Robert Lindsay, a son of the Earl of Balcarres, who succeeded as Resident or 'Collector' of Sylhet in 1778, four years after Thackeray left, grew quickly rich as a wholesale lime merchant and ship builder. 'My pay as Resident,' wrote the candid Robert, 'did not exceed £500 *per annum*, so that fortune could only be acquired by my own industry.' During the period of Thackeray's residence, from 1772 to 1774, there were not only similar contracts open to him, but also the profitable business of supplying elephants for the Company's troops.

These two men, William Makepeace Thackeray and the Hon. Robert Lindsay, are the first British administrators who left their mark in that remote District. They converted what had been a wild borderland into a British province, and 'Thackeray's House' was still pointed out when I visited Sylhet a century later. Their rule was a simple one. 'Black tax-farmers' brought the £17,000 of land-tax to the treasury in the local currency of cowries

—41,000 of which equalled one pound sterling. The British head of the District shipped off to Dacca the heaped-up masses of little shells; or kept part of them in payment for the lime, timber, and elephants which he supplied to the Company. Such local products formed in fact a means of remitting the revenue, alike profitable to the British Resident and convenient to the central Government. The Dacca Council asked few questions as long as the fixed amount of cowries, or their equivalent in the articles ordered for the Company, came down the river.

The serious business of the Resident of Sylhet, or 'Collector' as he began to be called in 1772, was to hold the District against the frontier tribes and rebellious chiefs. Each autumn the hillmen burst out upon the valley: if in any year they did not come, it was because the floods had already swept away the crops. Murderous affrays still took place between the Hindu and Musalman cultivators. At the greater festivals of the rival religions, temples were sacked, cows were slain within the holy precincts, mosques were defiled, and bloody reprisals followed on both sides. It must be remembered that when Thackeray went to Sylhet in 1772, it had only been under nominal British control for six years. He found it as it was left by centuries of native rule.

What that state was may be realized from a single incident in the administration of his near successor, the Hon. Robert Lindsay. On one festival, wrote this gentleman, having 'certain intelligence that the Muhammadans meditated an assault upon our Government,' and 'as the town was on fire in different directions, with my small force I marched to the place were the crowd was collected.' He found them drawn up at the top of a hill under command of a 'Priest,' and called on them to disperse. Their leader 'immediately drew his sword, and exclaiming with a loud voice, "This is the day to kill or to die—the reign of the English is at an end," aimed a heavy blow at my head. This I was fortunate enough to parry. But he struck so hard that my sword was broken, and little more than the hilt remained in my hand. My black servant at the same moment thrust a pistol into my hand, which I instantly fired and the Priest fell; and so close were we in contact that his clothes were set on fire. My sepoys in the rear, seeing my dangerous position, discharged a platoon while I stood in front, from which I miraculously escaped. We then charged with bayonets and drove the armed multitude over the hill.'

Lindsay reported the affair very simply to the Governor-General, Warren Hastings, saying that he did not expect any further strife, as those who would have continued it 'are no more.'

Thackeray, the first British 'Collector' of the District, found it in a still wilder state. Two of his sources of income were the destruction of tigers and the capture of wild elephants. Half a dozen years later, Lindsay continued to bag sixty or seventy tigers yearly, for which the Government allowed liberal rewards. Thackeray's name survives as a mighty hunter of elephants. Herds of these animals roamed through the mountains and forests, at times forcing the hillmen to lodge in trees for shelter, and sallying forth to devastate the villages and crop-lands of the plains. 'On visiting the country where the greater part of my elephants were caught,' wrote Lindsay, 'I fell in with a small tribe of hill people, living more in the style of the brute creation than any I had ever met with. They are well known by the name of Kukis, and have their habitations on spreading trees to defend them from beasts of prey. They live on wild honey and the fruits of the forest.'

If the supply of elephants for the Company's troops yielded a good profit, it was apt to bring the purveyor into unpleasant disputes. For the newly caught elephant is a delicate monster, apt to die on his travels, and with as infinite a capacity for unsoundness as a young horse. The difficulty of judging an elephant forms, indeed, the subject of many shrewd stories among the Bengal peasantry. One relates how a merchant who believed he had a really sound elephant, and was just about to complete its sale, espied a villager looking fixedly at the animal's hind legs. Fearing that the man detected some unknown flaw, he whispered, 'Say nothing till the bargain is struck, and I shall give you fifty rupees.' The villager stood silent and stolid as before, and presently the merchant handed him the money. 'But now tell me, what was it you discovered?' asked the merchant. 'Discovered? what could I discover?' replied the peasant, tying up the silver in his waistband. 'I had never seen an elephant before, and I was watching how far his tail could reach in flapping off the flies.'

In 1774 a batch of elephants, for which Thackeray was the real although not the ostensible contractor, turned out badly. Only sixteen out of sixty-six survived their trying march across India to Belgram —a distance of about a thousand miles. The price of the animals averaged Rs. 1000 each, and the Government, having given an advance of Rs. 33,000, disputed the balance and called on Thackeray to divulge his connexion with the nominal contractors. He refused, on the ground that if he were to do so, 'he might, by breaking his promise, forfeit the character of a man of principle and honour, and suffer in the opinion of his friends.' He preferred to bring the matter before a judicial tribunal, boldly sued the Company in the Supreme Court of Bengal, and obtained a decree for Rs. 29,600 (say £3,700) and costs.

The Court of Directors in England resented the loss. A couple of years after Thackeray had left India, they made it the subject of one of the carping despatches with which they rewarded the hard and faithful service of their Governor-General, Warren Hastings. The Bengal Government, it appears, had gone carefully into the matter, but did not find it possible to resist Thackeray's claim in court. Francis and his partisans, as usual, turned the action of the Governor into material for a malignant charge. But there can be little doubt that the pure-handed Hastings did his best in this as in other cases to see justice done. He himself, at an earlier period, held a contract for the supply of commissariat bullocks. Hastings had thus a personal knowledge of the very class of transactions in which Thackeray was engaged, and he knew perfectly what was permissible and what was not under the system of anonymous trade then practised in Bengal. His whole career, and especially his strict control as Governor-General, make it certain that if, in the interests of the Company, he could have defended the suit he would have done so.

The Hon. Robert Lindsay, indeed, did a much finer stroke of business in Sylhet. He found, four years after Thackeray's departure, the revenues still collected in cowries. A fleet of armed boats was maintained to convey this cumbrous currency of 700 millions of the little shells each year to Dacca, at 'a loss of no less than ten per cent., exclusive of depredations on the passage down.' The Honourable Robert conceived the idea of remitting the value of the cowries in limestone, for which he held the contract, and keeping the revenues of Sylhet in payment. It was only the unfortunate limit to the demand for mortar in Calcutta that prevented the whole land tax of the District from passing into his pockets. He also created a ship-building trade from the timber of the Sylhet forests, after some Crusoe experiences of being unable to get his craft down the river owing to their large size.

'I understand, my dear Robert,' wrote his mother the Countess of Balcarres, 'that you are a great ship-builder, and your talents in this line I do not dispute. But I have one favour to ask of you, which is that you will not come home in one of your own building!' 'I implicitly followed her advice,' adds the sagacious Robert.

During Thackeray's two years in Sylhet, he continued the native system of administration, but gradually imposed on it the methods of British rule. Under the Mughals an agent of the Delhi treasury, always distrusted and constantly changed, had remitted the revenue to Dacca, and made as much as he could by extortion during his precarious tenure of office. Village tax-farmers brought to the Emperor's intendant the quota payable by the separate rural communes, as shown in the books of the village accountant and the Imperial registrar. Each of these subordinates took in his turn an allowance, and increased it as much as he dared by bribes. The native Government recognized no landowners or intermediate proprietary rights between the Imperial fisc and the actual tillers of the soil. The rural community in Sylhet consisted of two classes, the officials and the cultivators.

In the early years of British rule the system began to be humanised by appointing the revenue-farmers from the chief occupiers of land. A class of quasi-proprietors thus grew up, with a stable interest in the good management of the District, representing the treasury demand on the one side and the actual capabilities of the rural communes on the other. In 1793 this class was sufficiently important to supply the basis of the Permanent Settlement of Sylhet. Under Thackeray and his immediate successors a number of oppressive imposts were abolished. The armed fleet against the river-pirates, for which a single division of the District had been mulcted in a tribute of forty-eight armed boats by the Mughal Governor, became a thing of the past. The District produced more revenue with less pressure upon the people. Deductions were frequently made for bad seasons and raids by the hillmen. But cultivation steadily extended, and the same area which sent £16,704 to the Mughal emperor in 1765, yielded £27,372 to the British Government in 1792. The land-tax continued to be paid in the shell-currency of cowries until 1820.

In 1774 Thackeray was promoted to be third in Council at Dacca, and rejoined his sister Jane and Major Rennell at that station. During this summer the three had to mourn for a little Jane, born to the Rennells in July, 1773. In time another little Jane took her place, and more children followed, but the parents never forgot that solitary grave in Eastern Bengal. A silver model of her tomb, made for the sorrowing mother, still remains an heirloom in the family.

This loss of their first-born, the common tribute paid by our predecessors in India for British rule, combined with Rennell's ill-health from wounds and fever to make them cast longing eyes homeward. There were no bracing Himalayan stations in those days. The Rennells got their only change of air by voyaging up and down the rivers in thatched country boats. Their sole sanitarium was the Chittagong coast-strip, backed by its low range of hills; now considered a malarious tract, then the one poor health-resort for our countrymen in North-eastern India. Writing thence in 1776, Rennell described it as the Montpelier of Bengal. That simple-minded philosopher found every place pleasant if his wife could only be with him. 'How supremely happy I am,' he says of Jane Thackeray, 'in possessing such a woman! Temper is, I believe, the basis of love and friendship. Neither the wittiest nor the wisest bear away the palm of happiness.'

Thackeray doubtless accompanied his sister and brother-in-law on these river journeys. The barge of the Third in Council would make a fine show among the little flotilla of roofed country pinnaces, with their green venetian windows and cooking-boats astern. But he, too, having accumulated a fortune, turned his thoughts towards home. In 1775 he paid a visit to Calcutta, and fell in love with a talented and beautiful girl. She was one of three sisters who, within a few years, married three Bengal civilians of note. Their father, Lieut.-Colonel Richmond Webb, born about 1715, and a cornet in the Queen's Own Royal Dragoons in 1735, became captain in Moreton's regiment in 1741, and commanded a company for King George at Culloden. He retired from the army as Lieutenant-Colonel in 1758, and was buried in the east cloister of Westminster Abbey in 1785.

This gallant officer sprang from a line of soldiers. The family originally bore the name of Richmond, and claimed descent from the De Richmonds, Constables of Richmond and Lords of Burton. Under their more modern surname of Richmond Webb, assumed upon marriage with the heiress of Draycot, Wilts, in the fifteenth century, they had during three hundred years given good men to the army and the State. Perhaps the most famous of them was General John Richmond Webb, the victor of Weynendal 1708, wounded at Malplaquet 1709, and a divisional commander in Marlborough's campaigns. One of his kinsmen, a captain in the Guards, died in 1734; leaving his property to an only son, Lieut.-Colonel Richmond Webb, whose daughter Amelia became engaged to Thackeray in 1775.

In that year Amelia Richmond Webb was a girl of seventeen, with a bright intelligence which set off Thackeray's more solid qualities and exercised an important influence on his after-life. The vestry book of St. John's Cathedral, Calcutta, records their marriage on January 31, 1776, and the young couple soon sailed for England. Thackeray had realized a competence by nine and a half years' work, and he preferred to retire in the first vigour of manhood rather than to pile up a fortune at the cost of broken health and domestic bereavement, such as overclouded his sister Rennell's home at Dacca.

Judging from the pay-sheets of Leadenhall Street, the Company got his services very cheap.

I have added together the annual salaries and allowances drawn by William Makepeace Thackeray throughout his ten years of Indian residence, as shown in the returns of the Bengal Government to the Court of Directors. The total for his entire service makes only Rs.16,230, or less than a single year's pay of a Bengal Collector of the lowest grade in the present century.

Even allowing for the higher value of the rupee, the sum would represent to Thackeray about £2,000, and might perhaps have sufficed for his necessary expenses during twelve months as a member of the Dacca Council. Such accounts, I have said, while they gave an appearance of marvellous economy to the Company's system of working, failed to show the incomes of their servants. I doubt if they disclose even their official pay. In ten years Thackeray saved enough to render him comfortable for the rest of his days. His fortune, like the larger ones carried home by many of his contemporaries, was acquired by private trade.

He and his bride were still very young and had long lives before them. She was but eighteen, he twenty-six, on their return to England in 1776. They found both her parents living; and the Richmond Webb family, with its ancient history, distinguished war-services, and the veteran of Culloden at its head, became an attractive feature in their home-life. We shall see the fascination which that lineage had for their grandson the novelist. They called their second son (his father) Richmond, and their next son Webb, names which took root among their descendants, and commemorate to this day their connexion with the feudal Constables of Richmond and the heiress of Draycot four centuries ago. Mrs. Thackeray's father, Colonel Richmond Webb, had only one son who grew to manhood, and he died as a young soldier, unmarried, in the American War. Of Colonel Richmond Webb's four daughters, the youngest did not marry. The other three, as already mentioned, became the wives of Bengal civilians.

One of these gentlemen, Mr. Peter Moore, a man of energy and talent, was destined to play an important part in the Thackeray family. As his brother-in-law the elephant-hunting Thackeray may be taken as the type of a Bengal District

Officer in the last century, so Moore represents the more brilliant career which the secretariat at the Capital held out to the abler or more fortunate members of that great service. Peter Moore reached Bengal at the age of sixteen, in 1769, three years after Thackeray, and the two youths were Writers together during a couple of years in Calcutta. In 1770 Moore was attached to the head-quarters of the Revenue Department as assistant under the Collector-General. Gaining a step in the following year, he was promoted in 1773 to the central office of control and appeal, which then began to gather into its hands the threads of the rural administration.

In this position, as assistant to the Superintendent of Khalsa, Calcutta, he mastered the new revenue system which Hastings was introducing into Bengal. That Governor-General had embarked on an investigation of the resources of Bengal, so as to put an end to excessive demands on the one side and to evasions or connivances on the other. He carried out his difficult task by a Committee of Revenue with himself at its head. In 1774 he appointed Peter Moore to be the secretary, and in 1776 to be a member of the Committee. In 1782 Moore reached the grade of 'Senior Merchant and Collector of the Assessment under the Rule of Ordnance,' to the shaping of which he had himself largely contributed. He apparently retired in 1783, with a fortune gained by fourteen years' service.

In 1774, when only twenty-one, he had married Sarah, eldest daughter of Colonel Richmond Webb, whose sister Amelia became the wife of Thackeray two years later. On returning to England Moore settled at Hadley, Middlesex—the 'faire plain for two armies to joyne together' made memorable by the battle of Barnet. There too the Thackerays bought a small property in January, 1786; perhaps with the help of Mrs. Thackeray's inheritance from her father, Colonel Richmond Webb buried in Westminster Abbey cloisters in June, 1785. The two married sisters, Sarah and Amelia, were thus reunited by the nearest ties of neighbourhood for the rest of their lives. Four years later, in 1790, Thackeray's own sister Henrietta also joined the little Bengal settlement at Hadley Green, after the death of her husband, James Harris. Thither, too, came often his other sister, Mrs. Rennell, and her now famous Major, who, on their retirement from India in 1777, had established themselves in the learned world of London, an hour and a half's drive from Hadley Green.

There is something very solid and English about this family party of sisters and brothers-in-law who, after a successful youth in India, settled down in early middle age to so close and affectionate an intercourse. Rennell brought to it the honours of a leading man of science, Moore formed a link between it and English public life, the Richmond Webb connexion added something of the gloss of fashion. Colonel Richmond Webb had given to his children a tone of chivalry and high yet practical aims which we are not wont to associate with the Georgian era. 'Be honest and good,' he wrote to his son while at Eton, the son whose career was destined to be cut short in the American War. 'You have a good stock of learning which I hope you won't neglect. Make yourself master of your fence and your sword, and you will be enabled to serve your King, Country, yourself and friends: and there's nothing that you, who are born a gentleman and educated like one, may not aspire to.'

The Thackeray household was perhaps the least distinguished of the Hadley group. While Rennell constantly scaled new heights in science, and Moore was making his mark in the Parliamentary and financial world, William Makepeace Thackeray led a simple but hospitable country life. A great digger in his garden, if nieces bantered him on his somewhat rural clothes, he replied, 'My dears, as I do not like the trouble of choosing, I tell my tailor to send me at one time this coloured suit, and at another a blue with brass buttons, so that when I write for a new one he looks in his order-book and sees which turn it is.' His portrait represents a generous, good-humoured face, with kind eyes, well-cut features, and a fresh colour. Thackeray's home was in keeping with its owner —'a quiet mead,' writes the family chronicler, 'with here and there fresh pools of water shining beneath clusters of fair lime trees.' Active in local good works and a steady churchwarden, the newspaper obituary of his twenty-seven years at Hadley Green dwells chiefly on the benevolence, integrity, and genial humanity which had made him the friend of all around.

Children soon began to fill the house, until in 1797 the tale of twelve was complete. Of the fortunes of some of them, the next chapter will speak. His wife's influence was the dominant one, and it imparted to the strong Thackeray character, racy of the Yorkshire moors, a finer blend from the Richmond-Webb descent. 'Those boys of William will be clever,' said his brother, himself an able man; 'they have such a clever mother.' She seems indeed to have been a bright, charming woman, with a certain graceful indolence and love of ease which sisters-in-law did not fail to mark, but benevolently ascribed to her having been in India. Amelia Thackeray died in 1810, aged fifty-three; and William Makepeace Thackeray, her husband, in 1813, in his sixty-fourth year.

The conspicuous member of the Hadley settlement was their brother-in-law, Peter Moore. The *Gentleman's Magazine* tells us that Moore 'made an ample fortune in India,' and as Lord of the Manor of Hadley, quartering the arms of the great Sir Thomas More, he took his place among the magnates of the neighbourhood. Barely thirty when he retired, he threw himself into English politics with the unabated energy which won his way in Bengal. He had owed his appointment in the Company's service to Lord Holland, and on his return home he became closely associated with the Whig leaders, acting for a time as a sort of unofficial whip. This connexion ranged him on the Burke and Sheridan side of the battle waged over Warren Hastings. In 1796 he was returned to Parliament along with Sir Philip Francis by the householders of Tewkesbury, but both were unseated on the ground that the franchise vested in the freemen and freeholders alone. Elected for Coventry in 1803, after a contest which cost him £25,000, Moore sat for that constituency through six Parliaments. In 1806 he had a son returned for Queenborough.

Politics, however, formed but one outlet for Moore's many-sided activity, and it would have been well for him if they had been the only one. He soon became prominent in the public ventures of the day. As chairman of the managing committee he took a leading part with Sheridan in the re-building of Drury Lane Theatre, and his town house formed a refuge at need for that spendthrift of talent. It was from Moore's residence in Great George Street that Sheridan's body was borne to Westminster Abbey, and it was he who placed the memorial above Sheridan's grave. The Manor House of Hadley became a centre for Whig politicians, and must have sorely tried the patience of its Tory neighbours. Moore figured as the chief projector of the Highgate Tunnel, the Imperial Gaslight Company, and in other speculations which the accumulation of capital after the long war set on foot. With a fine contempt for the cost of victory, he fought the famous battle of the Coal-gas against the Oil-gas Company, in which the latter dropped £30,000 and his side 'only £15,000!'

After representing Coventry for twenty-one years he lost his seat in 1824, as the silk-weavers suspected him of having favoured their masters' cause in a trade dispute. 'The Corporation or the Tory party took care to increase this suspicion,' says the *Gentleman's Magazine*, 'and by plying the electors with beer and gin carried the election.' Worse misfortunes awaited him. He had become conspicuous as 'one of the most adroit and successful men ever known' in getting a Company's bill through the House, and as a Company promoter in the inflation of 1824–5. When the collapse came, he gave up all his property beyond a bare subsistence. But although he had personally the reputation of honesty, he was 'made the scapegoat for a multitude of jobbers,' to again quote the *Gentleman's Magazine.* Compelled to fly to the Continent, as in England 'there was no hope of his last days being spent outside a prison,' he tried to write his memoirs at Dieppe, and died a broken exile at Abbeville on May 5, 1828, aged seventy-five.

Sir William Congreve, the inventor of the rocket which bears his name, was another scapegoat of the same crisis, and died in the same month a fugitive at Toulouse. Moore's ruined old age probably supplied some touches to the story of Colonel Newcome.

For perhaps the best service which he rendered to his country was his guardianship of his grandnephew, the future novelist. Thackeray's father died, as we have seen, at Calcutta in 1815; his mother married again; and when the little boy of six returned to England in 1817, his grandfather the elephant-hunter, and his grandmother, had been dead for some years. His grand-uncle Moore became his guardian, and the visits to the Manor House at Hadley formed some of the happiest recollections of Thackeray's childhood. The boy lived for a time, says a rather florid biographer who confounds the grand-uncle with the grandfather, 'amid the scent of his grandfather's clover, while he luxuriated in the indulgence which the old man lavished.'

Mr. Moore, his grand-uncle and guardian, was in fact the great man of Hadley throughout Thackeray's boyhood, overshadowing the other members of the family by his wealth, energy, and position in Parliament and in the financial world. Amid all his own speculations and calamities he guarded the little fortune left to the orphan. Thackeray on coming of age in 1832 found himself, we are told, in possession of £20,000.

But Moore's influence acted on the great novelist in a more permanent way. At the very age when the impressions of the boy harden and set into the memories of the man, Thackeray saw his guardian suddenly cast forth from the world of wealth and Parliament, and die an exiled bankrupt. The catastrophe formed his earliest awakening to the *Vanitas Vanitatum* which became the text of so much of his teaching: his first acquaintance with 'the old, old tale Of folly, fortune, glory, ruin.'

CHAPTER III

THACKERAY'S UNCLES IN INDIA

OF the twelve children born to Sylhet Thackeray and his wife eleven grew up, and nine found their way to the East. They at once became a great Indian family. The City influence of brother-in-law Moore doubtless helped to keep open the floodgates of patronage which so abundantly flowed from Leadenhall Street to the crowded household at Hadley Green. But that patronage was chiefly due to Sir Hugh Inglis, a 'private adventurer' or trader at Dacca during Cartier's residence there, 1754–1766. On Cartier's promotion to the Presidency town, ending with the Governorship of Bengal, Mr. Inglis followed him, and grew into one of the merchant princes of Calcutta. He thus came into close contact with Cartier's young friends, the Thackerays. Indeed the sagacious and kindly

Scotchman was one of 'the sensible men in India who were to find out Jane,' as her mother predicted. Retiring with a fortune in 1775, he was three times Chairman of the Court of Directors between 1797 and 1812, and received a baronetcy. Sir Hugh Inglis never lost sight of the old Dacca group, and as a lifelong friend of Jane Thackeray after her marriage to Rennell, he secured nominations for many of her nephews to the Company's service.

Of the seven sons of William Makepeace Thackeray three received appointments in the Company's Civil Service at Madras, a fourth in its Bengal Civil Service, and a fifth in its Bengal army. A sixth went to Calcutta as a barrister. Of four daughters who reached womanhood, two married Bengal civilians, the husband of a third was Attorney-General in Ceylon, the fourth became the mother of a distinguished member of the Viceroy's Council in India.

The only son of the Sylhet elephant-hunter who did not go to the East was Francis, in holy orders. A man of learning and of sufficient means, he early retired to a Hertfordshire parish and spent his life among his books. Famous in the family for his fairy tales, he gained an honourable place in the world of letters by his 'History of the Earl of Chatham' and his 'State of Ancient Britain under the Roman Emperors.' Carlyle repeatedly quotes Francis Thackeray's 'Lord Chatham' in his *Frederick the Great*. Lord Macaulay reviewed the work. M. Brunel includes it in his *Manuel du Libraire* among *les ouvrages les plus estimés en tout genre.*

If the fine Richmond-Webb strain showed itself in the fairy tales of Francis Thackeray, it took an erratic form in the youngest son Charles. Born in 1794, the child of his parents' mature middle life, Charles seems to have been the most brilliant of the brothers. Having been called to the bar he went to India to practise, but without the necessary licence. He returned to England to obtain one, and makes his appearance in a Directory of 1832 as one of the fourteen gentlemen who then constituted the Calcutta bar. Few legal loaves and fishes fell to Charles Thackeray's share. The Family Book speaks of him as 'full of wit and talent, handsome and agreeable—a victim to the demon of drink then so fashionable in India.'

An old Calcutta resident more vaguely described him as clever, fond of the bottle, and with little practice in his profession.

He found a congenial refuge on the Press, then bursting its official bonds, and asserting itself as a new power in India. When the versatile Stocqueler bought the *John Bull* and turned it into the *Englishman*, three barristers—John Peter Grant of an ancient Scottish family, John Farley Leith, and Charles Thackeray—were the leader-writers. The first two became famous names in Bengal: Charles Thackeray sank, about 1846, into an obscure grave. During the eight epoch-making years of the Afghan and Sikh wars which preceded his death, the *Englishman* was the voice of our countrymen in Bengal. Its leading articles not only recorded, but helped to create, history. The Indian sun makes no allowance for the frailties of genius. Charles Thackeray drifted into a waif. Yet some of the brightest articles in the newspaper which to this day leads British independent opinion in Bengal came from his pen. Lord Macaulay's last Essay, before sailing for India, was his review of Francis Thackeray's 'Earl of Chatham'

(January, 1834). During Charles Thackeray's years of Calcutta journalism, Macaulay set up at the *Englishman* press the rough proofs of yet more memorable Essays for the *Edinburgh Review.*

If official fortunes could still be made in India, they were on a small scale compared with the gains of private trade brought home by the preceding generation. The Company had long perceived the false economy of stinting their servants' pay, and allowing them to grow rich by traffic on their own account. But it was not till near the end of the last century that it nerved itself to apply the only real remedy—a fair day's wage for a fair day's work. During the years which intervened between Sylhet Thackeray's departure from India and the arrival of his sons in that country, the reform was carried out. Liberal salaries took the place of unrecognized profits, and an Indian civilian could only accumulate money by saving it from his monthly pay. For such modest fortunes heavy risks had still to be run. Of the six sons of Sylhet Thackeray who went to India, five died there, and the sixth on a voyage to the Cape for the recovery of his health.

The eldest of them, William Thackeray, born 1778, arrived at Madras as a Writer on January 3, 1796, a few months before he reached eighteen. After a year in the Secretariat he was sent as assistant to the Commercial Resident at Vizagapatam. There he set himself to learn the local dialect, and was the first Madras civilian who earned a reward under the rules of 1797 for encouraging the study of oriental languages. The examiners testified to his 'thorough and masterly knowledge of the Telugu,' for which the Government presented him, in 1800, with the sum of Rs. 3,500, then equal to about £400. He immediately received a good appointment, and an official minute assured him 'that should his attention to the duties of his new office be found equal to his diligence in the study of the language, the Governor in Council would have the same pleasure in promoting him in the Revenue Department which he then felt in bestowing the above public mark of approbation.'

Rapid advancement followed. Lord Clive, the Governor of Madras, appointed the young civilian of four years' standing to be Translator to the Government, and in November, 1800, selected him for a post of honour as an assistant to Sir Thomas Munro in the settlement of the territories just ceded to the Company by the Nizam. Thackeray's connexion with Munro gave him his chance in life. He won the regard of that great soldier-statesman, and under his training became himself one of the foremost administrators of his time.

In 1800 the Ceded Territories were handed over to us by the Nizam in a wild state: a state of constant battle between the peasantry and the petty military chiefs who squeezed them. Many of these local tyrants had been 'freebooters or leaders of banditti,' whom the distant Nizam bribed into his service by assigning to them the collection of the land-tax. Others had simply seized on patches of territory. A third section consisted of revenue agents who had thrown off their allegiance to the Nizam and stood out in revolt. A fourth and more merciful class claimed descent from the ancient Hindu Rajas of the country before the Nizam usurped it. Although in some cases their income did not exceed £50 a year, every chief kept up a mob of courtiers and military retainers who lived off the tillers of the soil.

Each of them, writes Sir Thomas Munro, 'became the leader of a little army, and carried on destructive feuds with the villagers immediately contiguous to him. Bands of robbers wandered through the country, plundering and murdering such travellers as refused to submit to their exactions. . . . It is computed that in the year 1800, when the Ceded Districts were transferred to the Company's rule, there were scattered through them, exclusive of the Nizam's troops, about 30,000 armed peons, the whole of whom, under the command of eighty poligars [or chieftains], subsisted by rapine, and committed everywhere the greatest excesses.'

The task assigned to Munro and his assistants was to bring order out of this chaos, and to substitute a fair revenue system for extortion by the sword. They spent their days in the saddle, and their nights in tents, ruined forts and Hindu temples, or under the shadow of some crumbling town-gate. One by one each hamlet was visited, and the people were assured that the British Government only asked for a moderate rental, and, in return, would protect them in the undisturbed possession of their homesteads and fields.

At first the news seemed too good to be true. In the old times when the villagers fled from their oppressors, the chieftain lured them back by similar promises, and even gave them an agreement in writing. 'But as soon as the crops were ready to be cut,' says the official record, 'he would seize the produce, breaking through his word without scruple.'

If the change seemed at first incredible to the peasants, the oppressors quickly perceived that to them it meant ruin. Their swarms of 30,000 armed retainers made the task of settling the country a dangerous one. The territory ceded to us in 1800 was a vast cauldron, a thousand miles in circuit, seething with armed violence and resistance. 'The ten years of Mughal government,' wrote Munro in February, 1801, soon after Thackeray joined him, 'have been almost as destructive as so many years of war, and this last year a mutinous unpaid army was turned loose during the sowing season to collect their pay from the villages. They drove off and sold the cattle, extorted money by torture from every man who fell into their hands, and plundered the houses and shops of those who fled.'

While assuring the peasantry of protection under British rule, Munro at the same time disarmed the chiefs. Their standing armies of freebooters were broken up, and those of the leaders who refused to settle down into quiet country-gentlemen were pensioned off or expelled. Munro had a sufficient force at his disposal, but like a true soldier he disdained military display in civil life. He and his assistants went about the country without escorts, rightly holding that a District Officer in India should depend on his own influence and the authority of his position for his personal safety, and that by the absence of guards 'we get much sooner acquainted with the people.'

This practice nearly cost William Thackeray's life. Hearing of a murderous affray in a fortified village near his camp, he hastened to the gate, was refused admittance, and tried to climb over the wall. His cool judgement saved him at the last moment, but Sir Thomas Munro was called on to explain how he allowed his assistant to be exposed without an escort to such dangers. Munro defended his refusal of escorts from the regular troops, and explained that Thackeray had a hundred armed police for keeping order in the territories assigned to his care. 'I shall give him three hundred more,' adds Munro with quiet humour, 'and he can select an escort from them, who will be sufficient for his protection if he does not try to scale forts!'

Three years under Munro laid the foundation of a friendship between the two men that lasted for life. Munro was seventeen years older than W. Thackeray, but they had a common ground in the scholarly pursuits which both loved. The soldier-statesman complained that his annual circuit of near a thousand miles, with its new set of urgent questions demanding settlement at each morning and evening camp, left him few moments for such studies. 'The hours I spend on horseback,' he wrote, 'are almost the only time I can call my own.' His halts at Thackeray's headquarters formed episodes in his tours to which he looked back in after years. Through many a glorious night the two men may have discoursed at the door of their tent, marching with Xenophon's Ten Thousand, or fighting over again, under the southern constellations, the Peloponnesian War.

Munro, from the time that he taught himself Spanish as a boy in order to read *Don Quixote*, and distinguished himself in the Glasgow University, had never lost his love of learning. William Thackeray was a good classic, and on his promotion to an independent charge, Munro wrote to him lamenting that an end had to come to their scholarly *causeries* in the jungle, and giving his young friend some characteristic advice.

'I regret your loss on my own account, for I used to enjoy a fortnight's halt at Adoni, and talking with you of Greeks and Trojans, after having seen nobody for perhaps three or four months before, but Bedars and gymnosophists. I hope that you will in your new government carry into practice the maxims of the Grecian worthies whom you so much admire; and that you will act in all situations as Aristides would have done; and when you feel your English spirits prompt you to act first and think afterwards, that you will recollect the temper of Themistocles—"Strike, but hear." You are not likely to be placed in exactly the same situation. But many others may occur, in the course of your Collectorate life, that will require as great a command of temper; and if there is any faith in physiognomy, I have no doubt that you will rival the Grecians. For, after you were cropt by the Adoni barber, you were a striking likeness of a head of Themistocles I recollect to have seen in an old edition of Plutarch's Lives, printed in the time of Queen Elizabeth.'

Since reference is thus made to William Thackeray's appearance, I may mention that he stood over six feet in height, and was famous for his horses and horsemanship. A portrait of him at this time, about the age of twenty-five, discloses a refined face with serious, soft, brown eyes under dark eyebrows. His wavy hair, long behind but cut straight across the forehead, suggests the Grecian likeness to which Munro refers.

Daily work among the chieftains and peasantry, who formed his sole companions except when Munro or some rare English officer rode into his camp, soon made Thackeray a master of his business. Within three years he thoroughly acquired Sir Thomas Munro's method of settling a newly ceded country. In 1803 he was called to apply it on his own account in an extensive southern chiefship including Tinnevelli to which he was appointed Collector. Soon afterwards he was promoted to be the first judge of the Court established at Masulipatam.

Another three years in that position enabled him to add a practical knowledge of judicial work to his training as a settlement officer. In 1806, Lord William Bentinck, the next Governor of Madras, determined to utilise for a difficult and delicate inquiry the double experience which W. Thackeray had thus gained. India was then in the throes of a great administrative crisis. The State-ownership of the soil had passed from the native Powers to the East India Company. How could the Company best exercise that ownership in the joint interest of itself and the people?

According to the old Indian practice, a practice with many and wide exceptions, the cultivators paid their rent direct, or through their headmen, to the Government officials. A countless army of tax-gatherers spread over the country, each underling squeezing as much as he could from the villagers, and sending on as little as he dared to the distant treasury. If the native dynasties failed to work such a system without oppression to the husbandmen, could the foreign British rulers hope to do so? The best chance of protecting the people, and of securing the land-revenue, seemed to good authorities to evolve a body of intermediate proprietors—men of substance who would be responsible for the revenue to the Government, and at the same time have an hereditary interest in the welfare of the cultivators.

This view prevailed in Bengal, and was embodied in the Permanent Settlement of 1793. The Court of Directors desired its extension to other provinces. But the rural conditions of Madras were different from those of Bengal. In many districts of southern India the old village communes survived with sufficient vitality to protect the peasants. To set up intermediate owners between them and the Government would merely create a new machinery of oppression and a new charge to be squeezed out of the cultivator. Lord William Bentinck found himself surrounded by zealots for both the rival systems; one party urging a permanent settlement with proprietors of our own making, another party insisting upon a peasant settlement year by year. The Home authorities pressed for a decision. Bentinck looked round for some calm-headed and experienced man to inquire into the actual facts, and chose William Thackeray for the duty.

It was not an easy duty. His decision, whatever it might be, would give offence to the one side or the other, and be bitterly attacked. Thackeray reported with a fairness and a fullness of knowledge which won Lord William Bentinck's gratitude. The Governor not only endorsed his views, but he resolved to give his adviser a position which would enable him to carry them out. In 1806 he nominated William Thackeray, then only thirty, to be a member of the Board of Revenue, defending the appointment of so junior a member of the service in a minute from which I take the following sentences. It forms an example, happily common in India, of a young man being raised to high office without personal influence, and simply on the record of his work.

'I was introduced to the acquaintance of this officer by the reputation of his character and ability, and from the good opinion which further inquiry led me to entertain of him. I was induced to ask the permission of Council that I might have his assistance in determining how far a change in the principle of the Permanent Settlement might be advisable. Mr. Thackeray has greatly aided me in this investigation, and in the course of our communication I have observed in him much information, the powers of sound reasoning, and great benevolence. Attaching as I do the greatest consequence to this question, and feeling that it will equally tend to the great amelioration of the condition of the mass of the people and to the progressive increase of the revenues of the Company, I am anxious that there should be in the Board of Revenue a member possessing the same sentiments with myself. The life, both natural and political, of an individual in India is very precarious, and I should be sorry that with mine this discussion should die also. I found in Mr. Thackeray the sentiments which I entertained: they were not adopted from me. They were the result of his own observation.'

It thus fell to William Thackeray to play a leading part in the land-settlement on which the future of southern India depended, and upon which the rights of the people still rest. Lord William Bentinck soon employed his young member of the Board in a new field. In each part of the country the settlement was preceded by a grand inquest or Domesday book, recording all rights connected with the ownership and cultivation of the soil. In this inquest for eastern and central Madras Thackeray had won his reputation. That reputation he was now to mature as sole commissioner in the inquiry on the western coast. If we sometimes marvel at our success in India, it is in part because we overlook the patient labour which built it up. The following instructions of Lord William Bentinck to Thackeray in November, 1806, show the care taken to secure that the Indian Domesday should supply a complete record of the facts before the form of settlement was decided.

'It is the intention of his Lordship in Council that you shall proceed in the first instance to the province of Kanara, and having completed the inquiry entrusted to you in that province, you will prosecute similar researches in the neighbouring province of Malabar, whence you will visit the

Ceded Districts for the purpose of perfecting your investigation.

'The objects of your research will be to ascertain the present state of each province. The sources of its revenue, especially the land-revenue. The principle on which the assessment on the land is formed. The question of produce payable by the land-holders. The security taken for the due collection, and the mode of collecting the land-revenue. The nature of land-tenures, the right of the land-holders. The state of agriculture, the state of the police and of the administration of justice as far as it affects the revenue. The defects, if any, of the present revenue management. . . . The condition, opinions, and wants of the cultivators. The present state of the country in respect to the comfort of the people. The amount and security of the revenue compared with other times and governments.

'To the result of these inquiries you will add your opinion on the best mode of administering the revenue in future, and the mode of introducing the Permanent Settlement in particular. You will discuss fully every part of this subject with the local revenue servants, and you will communicate freely with the people.' If the British settlement of India, unlike the Norman settlement of England, proved a basis of security instead of an instrument of oppression to the subject races, it is partly because our Indian Domesday book concerned itself not more with the interests of the Crown and the landholders than with the rights of the tillers of the soil.

William Thackeray's answers to the questions thus proposed by Lord W. Bentinck have passed into history. They form part of the evidence submitted to Parliament in 1812, with a view to deciding on what terms the Company's charter should be renewed. William Thackeray did not possess the literary charm of style granted to several of his brothers, and in so abundant a measure to his illustrious nephew. His reports give in scrupulous detail an exact record of what he himself observed, and of the conclusions at which he himself arrived. Although trained by Sir Thomas Munro in the Peasant Settlement school, and afterwards associated with him in giving legislative effect to its principles, Thackeray carefully notes the existence of superior tenures and proprietary rights wherever he found them. His report of 1807 received high praise from the Madras Government and the Court of Directors, and survives to this day as a model of painstaking and impartial inquiry.

Such an inquiry formed in itself an administrative education to the officer who conducted it. The Malabar coast had an unique historical interest, and disclosed a conflict of rights based on the claims of successive races to the soil. The 'Malé whence the pepper comes' of Cosmas Indicopleustes and the Greeks, Malabar was also the scene of the early Arabian trade with India and of the first Portuguese settlements. A series of exquisite lagoons fringed with tropical vegetation stretch along the coast; behind them rises a mountain wall 3,000 to 5,000 feet in height. Its mighty buttresses of precipice and forest, the haunt of the tiger and the bison, also formed the retreat of once powerful but then crushed races. On this ancient coast W. Thackeray had to mediate between land-rights, some of them descended from the primaeval hunting tribes, others from the dim period of the shepherd kings, overlaid not only by the claims of a military caste and a Hindu theocracy, but also by a Christian community imagined to be as old as St. Thomas, and certainly dating from the patriarchs of Antioch. A fierce Musalman population of Moplas, left behind by the early Arab commerce, constantly broke out in partly agrarian and partly fanatical risings.

The country passed under British rule in 1791, and the generation which had grown up in the state of anarchy still survived when Thackeray came upon the scene. Perhaps the most interesting class whose rights he had to reconcile with the claims of others were the Nairs. This soldier race still practised the primitive form of marriage known as polyandry, by which a woman may have several husbands, and property descends by inheritance not to a man's sons but to his sister's children. A Malabar drama recounts with much humour the quarrels between the five husbands of a Nair lady, ending with their return to domestic concord.

While William Thackeray was studying this congeries of races, and mediating between them, he was sapping his own constitution. The malaria of the coast strip and hill jungles laid hold of him with a grip that he never shook off. In 1810 he was promoted to be Chief Secretary to the Madras Government, but after struggling for three years under medical treatment, he had to be sent home for the recovery of his health in 1813. The court of Directors cordially recognized his services in a despatch, and again on his return to India in 1816.

After intermediate appointments, including the charge of two important Districts, he was deputed in 1818 to the northern Madras frontier of Ganjam, says the official record, 'to report on the best means of establishing permanent tranquillity.' Again he laid out the lines on which a wild territory was to be brought under peaceful administration, and received as reward a judgeship in the High Court of Madras. By the age of forty William Thackeray had thus impressed his personality on the settlement of three great areas of southern India; from its south-western coast, through its central districts, to its northernmost province.

In 1820 Sir Thomas Munro returned to India as Governor of Madras. In terms of the Court of Directors' despatch, laying down the new constitution of government, William Thackeray was appointed a provisional member of Council, and took his seat on June 10, 1820. Three days later he also became President of the Board of Revenue, or executive head of the internal administration. But he did not long enjoy his honours in Council, or his renewed companionship with his old friend Munro. In November, 1822, he had again to fly for life, but proposed only a trip to the Cape of Good Hope, whence he trusted 'in a few months to return to the public service.' He died upon the voyage on Jan. 11, 1823, aged forty-four years and eight months.

The whole Presidency lamented his loss. Sir Thomas Munro recorded a last tribute to 'his integrity and long, zealous, and able services.' The Government went into public mourning for fourteen days. A Gazette extraordinary ordered 'that the flag of Fort St. George be immediately hoisted half staff high, and continue so until sunset this evening, and that minute guns, forty-seven in number, corresponding to the age of the deceased (*sic*), shall be fired from the ramparts of Fort St. George.' William Thackeray's true memorial is to be found in the great State Papers which he wrote, and in the prosperity of the provinces to which he brought justice and peace.

The careers of his two younger brothers in the Madras Civil Service were much shorter ones. Webb Thackeray arrived as a Writer in 1806, at the age of eighteen. He died within a year, but not before he had won notice for a clever little grammar of the Hindustani language in verse. His first six months of service were passed as assistant in the Board of Revenue at head-quarters, his second six as Assistant in the Belary District. He died at the mouth of a mountain pass while he was being carried to the coast in the hope of benefit from the sea-air. His chief lamented his loss in a letter to the Government not only for 'the very great assistance' which the poor youth had been able to render him, but also as an officer 'possessed of the finest disposition,' and of a facility in corresponding in the Hindustani language described as 'wonderfully great.'

The next brother in the Madras Civil Service was St. John Thackeray, born 1791. Arriving in 1809, as one of the first civilians sent out by the East India College which grew into Haileybury, St. John Thackeray spent his first three years in the Board of Revenue and in the diplomatic or 'Political' Department of the Government. Five more years of District work completed his training, and in 1818 he was chosen, in flattering terms, to help to bring into order the territories just won from the Marathas. It seemed, indeed, to be the common lot of the Thackerays to introduce the British administration into newly annexed provinces.

For that work St. John Thackeray paid the price of his life. The loyal chief of Kittúr died in 1824, leaving no issue. The usual family intrigues followed. A deed of adoption was forged; the insurgent party seized the Kittúr fort and defied our Government. To save bloodshed St. John Thackeray advanced unguarded with a flag of truce on October 23, 1824, and was killed. His gallantry and self-devotion form an example of that calm civil courage which has acted like a spell in each new province of British India. The Government despatch speaks of his death 'as a public calamity.' In the reduction of the fort another District Officer, the nephew of Sir Thomas Munro, was also slain.

The two Thackeray brothers who had entered the Bengal Service were already in their graves.

Of Richmond, the great novelist's father, the next chapter will speak. Thomas Thackeray, eighth child of the Sylhet elephant-hunter, was appointed an Infantry cadet in 1803, at the age of fourteen. Promoted to a lieutenancy in 1805, and never rising above that grade, he served long enough to leave behind the most striking picture that exists of a Bengal regiment in the old time of British conquest, and to die a hero's death.

'I am at great pains,' he wrote, 'to fill up the vacancies which occur in my company by brothers of the best sepoys, and seldom entertain a recruit who is not in some way related to a man already in the company. I have succeeded so well that I have now four full brothers of one family, three of another, and out of ninety men I have not twenty who are not connected, either by consanguinity or marriage, with some of their comrades. Men naturally become attached to the service in which they have so many ties.' A Bengal regiment thus formed a family fighting force of the military and Brahman castes, recruited and handled by captains or lieutenants with a freedom of initiative which a colonel-commandant would now envy.

In 1814 Lieutenant Thomas Thackeray took part in the Nepal War. Badly wounded while storming a frontier fort in October, he managed to scrawl a message home, 'Don't be afraid; I'm very little hurt.' Then, with his left hand, a couple of months later: 'The day after I was wounded I received your letter of the 17th of April, which gave me more pleasure than my wound gave me pain.' He hopes that 'very shortly my right hand will be able to apologize for this awkward attempt of my left to express my affection for all of you, my dear sisters and brothers.'

The right hand was never to apologize. Despite its disablement, Lieutenant Thackeray insisted on going into action. On December 27, 1814, our troops were driven back from a Nepalese stockade. He volunteered to cover their retreat with his Light Company against, says the record, 'a strong and overpowering column of Gurkhas.' Nine times he charged the enemy, and eight times he stopped their pursuit. In the ninth, his company seems to have fairly cut its way through their line, and was surrounded by their whole force. Thackeray and his gallant ensign fell, with fifty-seven of his brave sepoys. The regiment rescued his body, and, defying every rule of caste, testified their admiration for their champion by themselves carrying his corpse to the grave.

Nor were statelier tributes wanting in high places. 'Justice to extraordinary valour,' wrote the head of the army, 'demands from the Commander-in-chief the recorded expression of his unfeigned regret at the loss the service has sustained in the fall of Lieutenant Thackeray.' 'The heroic conduct of the Light Company, 2nd Battalion, under the command of Lieutenant Thackeray,' runs the Government of India's Despatch, 'demands the peculiar and recorded tribute of the Governor-general's approbation and applause. His Lordship deeply laments the untimely fate of Lieutenant Thackeray, and the brave officers and men who perished with him, in the performance of the most heroic acts of devotion to the cause in which they were engaged.'

I have said that the Calcutta graveyards are strewn so thick with heroes as to leave small space for separate monuments. So each frontier of British India is traced out with the tombstones of our gallant dead, for whom there was no time to write epitaphs. The sole memorial of Lieutenant Thomas Thackeray on the Heights of Jeytuck is the mention of his name on a slab to his brave ensign, Wilson, who died with him.

The careers of the six Thackeray brothers disclose a great Indian family in an aspect perhaps little realized. We think of such families as prosperous cliques who, apart from personal merit, were pitch-forked into a lucrative service, and retired without effort to various degrees of opulence. The walls of our parish churches record many such lives; a few are commemorated in our abbeys and cathedrals. But we forget that they were the survivals, not of the fittest, but of the most fortunate. The accurate Rennell computed in the last century 'that scarce one out of seventy men returns to his native country.' This sketch of the Thackeray brethren shows what became of the rest. Not under cathedral roofs nor in any consecrated ground, wrote the noble Dalhousie on his tablet to a young civilian and soldier who met death hand-in-hand, but amid the jungles or on the furthest frontiers of India lie our heroes who died doing their duty.

CHAPTER IV

THACKERAY'S FATHER IN BENGAL

RICHMOND THACKERAY, father of the novelist and second son of the Sylhet elephant-hunter, was born, according to the Family Book, on September 1, 1781. Sent to Eton in 1791, at the age of ten, he remained there till 1796, and received a nomination to the Company's Civil Service through the influence of his Aunt Rennell's friend, [Sir] Hugh Inglis. After the usual training in merchants' accounts he sailed for Bengal in his seventeenth year. His arrival as Writer in the Calcutta records bears date October 27, 1798. But he was almost immediately struck down by one of the maladies which lie in wait for newcomers at the close of the rains, and the doctors sent him off on a health voyage to Madras.

There he hoped to meet his eldest brother, William, who had been settled in the Southern

Presidency since 1796. Instead of a hospitable welcome and a quiet home, he found Madras in the full blast of preparations for the Mysore War, and his brother transferred to Vizagapatam, several hundred miles up the coast. 'My dear Mater,' Richmond wrote to his mother on February 17, 1799, 'it is intensely hot and I am obliged to go out in the sun. There are no palankeens here, for the bearers are all gone with the army, which has taken the field.' He wistfully pictures to himself his mother's 'routs going on at Hadley as they were last winter,' and 'Pater digging with Old Anthony' at the flower beds. 'I would give anything to be at home. I would even be glad to carry gravel in a basket on my shoulder in the garden! It was this time last year we made the new walk: it will be wonderfully altered when I see it again!' The poor lad was not to see it again. He lies for ever by a coarse brick path in a land where no gravel is.

From his first illness Richmond Thackeray in due course recovered, and returned to Calcutta. There he studied for a time in the College of Fort William, which Lord Wellesley founded with magnificent intentions in 1800. Richmond Thackeray, like his brothers, seems to have been clever at languages. He took a first-class in Arabic, with distinction in Persian, and was appointed assistant to the 'Collector' or chief of Midnapur, then a frontier tract of Lower Bengal. Although still open to predatory incursions, the British borderlands had been tamed since his father hunted elephants in Sylhet. With the Permanent Settlement in 1793, the heroic age of District administration passed away. The landholders' status became one of right instead of favour, their armed retinues gave place to a police, courts of law superseded and controlled the personal rule of the British Collector.

The year of Thackeray's arrival, 1798, marked also the commencement of the Governor-Generalship destined to consummate this change. The Marquis of Wellesley brought to his task an imperious will such as India had not felt since the days of Clive, and an authority more ample than even Clive found it possible to enforce. Lord Wellesley's rule completed the reform of the Civil Service, and transmuted District life in Bengal from poetry to prose. Little of the picturesque or epical can therefore be expected in Richmond Thackeray's service. The elephant-catching and ship-building ventures of his father were gone for ever.

Nevertheless, there was still hard work to be done. The Collector of Midnapur, as Warden of the Marches, held in check the wild highlands on the west, and the Maratha province of Orissa on his southern border. The hill-country, now known as the Tributary States, formed a tangle of inaccessible gorges and forests under primitive tribal sway, or split up among Hindu fort-holders who had wedged themselves in among the non-Hindu ancient clans.

To some of these clans immemorial custom prescribed that a state of war must always be presumed against all neighbours with whom there was not at the moment an express truce. The flesh and bones of human sacrifices were yearly ploughed into the furrows, in honour of the Earth-Goddess, at the spring festival. Others still used the flint arrow-heads of the stone age. Certain tribes, 'the Leaf Wearers,' were for the first time clothed with cotton strips at a solemn gathering held by their British officer in our own times.

During the years preceding Thackeray's arrival in Midnapur, that District had formed the theatre of stirring events. 'Violences of the Rajas,' 'inroads by the Marathas,' 'confiscations of lands,' 'depredations' and 'disturbances' of many kinds, are not infrequent headings in my excerpts from the manuscript records. But at the beginning of the present century the British Government took this outlying tract sternly in hand. The Marathas had scourged our Midnapur border to the north of their Orissa province with whips: Lord Wellesley chastised them with scorpions. The Company's factory on the Midnapur frontier, notwithstanding reinforcements of troops, was subjected to a series of 'acts of violence.' Indeed, the Marathas had devastated right across the District to the Hugli estuary, and turned a favourite river-resort of Warren Hastings into an absolute waste. In 1803 Lord Wellesley sent an army into Orissa, drove out the Marathas, and annexed the province to British India.

Richmond Thackeray's first years of work were the ones immediately preceding this *dénouement*. He learned the routine of a young District Officer, superintending the collection of the revenue, selling up landholders who refused to pay, and settling their allowances, embanking rivers, bringing under assessment estates which had evaded taxation, breaking up robber gangs, and looking after the Company's salt-manufacture along the coast. He played a very subordinate part, and for a brief period, in Midnapur; but he seems to have given satisfaction to his superiors. In 1802, after being transferred for a short time to his father's old District of Dacca, he was appointed assistant to the Secretary of the Board of Revenue, Calcutta, and to the Persian and Bengali translator.

In 1802, also, with the strong family affection which breathes in the letter from Madras to his mother, Richmond Thackeray, like his father before him, made a home for two sisters, Emily and Augusta. They did not, however, remain long with him. In 1803 Emily married at Calcutta a young civilian, John Talbot Shakespear, with whom she was destined to share a brilliant career. Shakespear, after figuring in the prize-lists of the College of Fort William, was in 1803 appointed assistant to the Collector of Birbhum, an office held, as we shall see, in that year by his brother-in-law Richmond Thackeray. Augusta also married a civilian, Mr. Elliot, 'her brother's dearest friend.'

Of Emily Shakespear's nine children who grew up, eight entered the civil or military service of the East India Company or married officers in these services. Her eldest son, Colonel John Dowdeswell Shakespear, a noble, chivalrous figure, was believed in the family to have formed the original of 'Colonel Newcome.' Her second daughter, Augusta, was the wife of General Sir John Low, who crowned his splendid services in camps and courts as British Resident in Oudh during the critical years preceding its annexation. 'No man,' wrote Kaye, 'knew the temper of the natives better. He could see with their eyes, speak with their tongues, and read with their understandings.'

Another son was Colonel Sir Richmond Shakespear, who in 1840 obtained deliverance for the Russian prisoners in Central Asia, and in the following year rescued our own ladies and children from captivity after the annihilation of the British force in the Afghan snows. But it were long to follow the several careers of that gallant brotherhood, in each one of whom blended the strength and gentleness which make the flower of manhood. Of this Colonel Sir Richmond Shakespear, his cousin Thackeray says in one of his *Roundabout Papers*:

'"Can I do anything for you?" I remember the kind fellow asking. He was always asking that question of kinsmen; of all widows and orphans; of all the poor; of young men who might need his purse or his service. His purse was at the command of all. His kind hand was always open. It was a gracious fate which sent him to rescue widows and captives. Where would they have found a champion more chivalrous, a protector more loving and tender?'

Emily Thackeray was not unworthy to be the mother of such sons. Her journal, jotted down for her children at school in England, discloses the clear eyesight and rapid realistic style which seem to have been the common inheritance of the Thackerays in that generation. Here is a little vignette, one of hundreds, dashed off while she and her husband were accompanying the Governor-General, Lord Moira, on his tour of 1814. The grandiose Anglo-Indian life of that time rises in a moment before us. We embarked, she writes, in a 'fleet of four hundred boats, which made a gay and brilliant display on the river Hugli. The State barge was painted green, richly ornamented with gold. Another pinnace, of equal dimensions and almost equal beauty, was appropriated to the use of his lordship's children, and a third, *The Castle,* was a banqueting and audience boat. A splendid barge for the reception of the band, and a large vessel fitted up with all the conveniences of a kitchen, were also in attendance, all of them painted green, with gilt mouldings to match the State pinnace. We dined with his lordship on board *The Castle.* The band of Her Majesty's 44th Regiment played during the evening on the barge, which was anchored near us.'

Emily Thackeray, like all her six brothers who went to India, died there; her husband also died on his voyage from Calcutta to the Cape of Good Hope, and was buried at sea.

In the year of Emily's marriage, 1803, Richmond Thackeray was sent as officiating Collector to another frontier District, Birbhum, on the west of

Lower Bengal. In Bengal as in Madras, from the elephant hunter of Sylhet downwards, the Thackerays seemed destined to the charge of newly annexed or border tracts. But the authorities at head-quarters did not lose sight of Richmond, and his work in the provinces was pleasantly intermitted by advancement in the central Board of Revenue at Calcutta.

Birbhum, his first independent charge, consisted of two ancient principalities, which had been reduced with some difficulty during the preceding half-century. It lay on the north of his former District Midnapur, and then included a lowland tract bordering on the Gangetic valley on the east, together with a vast region of forests and highlands rising westwards towards the Central Provinces.

The four years, 1803–1807, during which Thackeray remained, with some intervals, in charge of it, are memorable for the breaking up of the old frontier Houses of that part of Bengal. The Musalman Raja of Birbhum, the descendant of the hereditary Wardens of the Marches under the Mughal Empire, died in 1802, leaving his estates in ruin, and his family to the bounty of the British Government.

Thackeray found the yet more ancient Hindu Rajas of Bishnupur, which formed the southern part of the District, in an equally sorrowful plight. The hill Raja of Panchet on the west, with his jungle territory of nearly 3,000 square miles, had also fallen into arrears of revenue, and suffered the indignity of the attachment of his lands, and the arrest of his person for debt.

The truth is that the old ruling families of the frontier played too long at keeping up the style of semi-independent princes after they had, in reality, passed from feudatories into subjects. They could not bear to part with their courtly pomp and armed retinues. The Musalman Raja of Birbhum had shut himself up in his fort, because custom forbad him to go forth except at the head of his household cavalry, and the horses were either dead or too starved to bear their riders. The Hindu Rajas of Bishnupur boasted of an unbroken pedigree through some sixty generations from 715 A.D., with a semi-divine progenitor in the still more distant background. A native chronicler describes their capital, with its walls seven miles in length, as 'more beautiful than the beautiful house of Indra in heaven.' When Thackeray took charge of the District, one mangy elephant chained under a tree, and a monster rusty cannon ten feet and a half long, formed the sole relics of their ancient magnificence. Even the family idol had been pawned to a money-lender in Calcutta.

The great famine of 1770 had put the last touch to their ruin. When the local records open, the young Birbhum Raja scarcely passed the first year of his majority before being confined for debt; the venerable Raja of Bishnupur, after years of weary duress, was let out of custody only to die. The Company had, in fact, ceased to desire from them the military service by which they held their territories under the Mughal Emperors. What it wanted was revenue, not troops. Such of the ancient border Houses as could not accommodate themselves to the change had, up to 1793, been from time to time dispossessed of their estates, while their personal property was sold for arrears of the land-tax. The Permanent Settlement in that year, although giving to solvent proprietors a status which they never before enjoyed, provided a sharp remedy for those who still insisted on spending their rental on military pomp instead of paying the due quota into the District treasury. Under its provisions, estates which fell into arrears were sold by public auction.

This was the condition of Birbhum when Richmond Thackeray took charge of it in 1803. One of the questions he had to deal with was the subdivision of his vast frontier jurisdiction—far too large for effective control by a single chief. In 1805 the Legislature separated its western region into a new administrative District, called the Jungle Tracts.

The small fief-holders who held the passes between the hill-country and the lowlands of Birbhum had run the same course as their over-lords the Rajas. The Company, having imposed peace on the border, no longer needed the feudal defences, and tried to resume or assess the lands assigned for that purpose. Hence subterfuges and resistance, secret transfers, defaults, arrests of the petty chieftains of the passes, and forced sales of their property: a huge imbroglio, in the midst of which Thackeray found himself plunged. For a time it seemed as if the whole watch and ward on the frontier would join with the criminal classes in a confederacy of plunder. Thackeray did his share in bringing about a better state of things. But several Collectors spent their energies on the task before order could be evolved. The old guards of the passes were gradually transformed into an inefficient rural police, paying a quit-rent for their military grants of land.

The perplexities of a debased currency, malpractices by his official underlings, the devastations of river-floods, and depredations by gang-robbers, occupied the leisure moments of Richmond Thackeray in Birbhum. But the tide had already turned. A more enterprising class of proprietors were settling on the broken-up estates of the feudal aristocracy, and the work of reconstruction began. The provision of allowances for dispossessed landowners ceased to be a main duty of the Collector; new problems arose out of the extended cultivation going on all around. Thackeray impressed his personality on his subordinates, and was long remembered as the hospitable head of the District. An aged cook, whose recollections I noted down in Birbhum in 1864, still spoke of the generous kitchen of 'Tikri Saheb.'

In 1804–5 Thackeray took charge for a short time of the District of Tipperah, on the opposite or eastern frontier of Bengal, and became Sub-Secretary to the Board of Revenue at Calcutta. Returning to Birbhum in 1806, he was appointed Judge of Ramgarh, then a wild, outlying tract of hill and forest valleys to the west of Birbhum, but now one of the great coal-fields of Bengal. In 1807 he received the reward of his District work by promotion to the Secretaryship of the Board of Revenue, which controlled from the capital the general administration of Bengal. In 1808 he officiated as Judge of Midnapur, thus returning as head of the District to the scene of his first labours.

With the interval of his judgeship at Midnapur, he seems to have resided from 1807 in Calcutta. As Secretary to the Board of Revenue he held a considerable place in the official and social life of the capital. The years during which he was at the Board preceded the Parliamentary inquiry that abolished the Company's Indian trade and threw it open to the nation. But although many questions of the first importance passed under review, Thackeray's position as Secretary merged his individuality in the collective proceedings of the Board. On the other hand, we catch glimpses of him in contemporary journals, flitting in a genial and even sparkling fashion through the Calcutta gaieties of the time.

In 1807, for example, he appears in the *Calcutta Gazette*, with the Honourable Mountstuart Elphinstone and two other young civilians, as giving a 'masqued ball of peculiar splendour.' 'The rooms, overspread with green and flowery foliage,' wrote the local Jeames, 'presented a scene of rural beauty,' and before half-past ten were filled with 300 masqueraders. Among them 'a quack doctor anxious to dispose of his medicines, which had the singular property of curing the diseases of the mind,' directed his harangues 'chiefly to the female part of his audience, whom he professed to cure of their propensity to scandal.' 'An ambassador from the Emperor of Morocco--a capital mask at least ten feet high attended by his armour-bearer, a dwarf.' 'A nurse, with a babe in leading strings measuring about six feet high. This amiable infant managed its rattle with great address.'

And so on through a quaint list. The band of

Her Majesty's 67th Regiment made music to which the more stately of the company danced in costumes of many ages and nations. But the fun seems to have been rather rougher than we are now accustomed to. 'A ghost about twelve feet high was encountered by a Jack-tar, who mistook his night-cap for a mainsail, which Jack instantly proceeded to reef.' A barber tried to forcibly shave 'a tailor sitting cross-legged on his shop-board'—'a most active tradesman' was this artist in soap-suds, 'though we cannot in conscience recommend him as a very safe and careful operator.'

The sale-list of 'the elegant property of Richmond Thackeray, Esq., about to leave the Presidency,' January, 1806, when re-transferred to Birbhum, also appears in the *Calcutta Gazette*. It suggests a somewhat magnificent style of life for a young civilian of seven years' service. A little armoury of guns, swords, 'Persian scimitars and poniards, in velvet scabbards very richly mounted in silver'; five high-class horses, including 'the young, very active and highly dressed, light grey Arab saddle-horse *Nimble*,' of 'a fine generous temper'; with 'a handsome Europe-built coach lined with yellow cloth'; and 'very fashionable Household Furniture in white and gold,'—would have satisfied the aspirations of most bachelors just turned twenty-four. But Richmond Thackeray also cultivated the arts and *belles lettres* with the aid of 'a large Mahogany Box of Reeves's colours, with silver mountings; an excellent library of books; and very fine statues in plaister of Paris.' 'Ackermann's collection of beautiful Engravings for 1804–5, exquisitely coloured and highly finished in large vellum folios, richly gilt and lettered, imported on one of the last ships, and cost upwards of 100 guineas,' shows that the youthful virtuoso was quite up to date.

He seems, indeed, to have been a young gentleman of many tastes. 'A capital patent Saloon Organ, with fine barrels of the latest and most approved tunes, having the flageolet, tabor drum, triangle, diapason principal, twelfth and flute stops,' discoursed music for lady guests at 'his house in Chouringhee.' 'Valuable Paintings, Prints, and Convex Mirrors, in rich burnished gold frames' adorned its walls—and are set forth in the choice language of the Calcutta auctioneer.

Needless to say that the owner of all these fine

things figures in the functions with which India, then as now, welcomed the coming and sped the departing Governor-General. He formed one of the Committee appointed to draw up the famous farewell address from 'the British inhabitants of Calcutta' to Lord Minto; and altogether appears as a considerable personage in the social and public life of the capital.

In 1810 he married at Calcutta one of the reigning beauties of the day. He himself had an attractive personality, and his picture, which hangs in the drawing-room of his grand-daughter the authoress of *Old Kensington*, resembles the striking portrait of his Madras brother, William, already described. 'It is that of a very young man in an old-fashioned dress and brass buttons,' writes this lady, 'and white handkerchief round his neck; with brown hair falling loose, with bright soft hazel eyes and arched black eyebrows. The face is long and narrow, the nose is long, the complexion is clear, the mouth delicate and yet not without a certain determination and humour. The eyes have a peculiar out-looking depth of expression which I remember in my Father' [the

Novelist]. 'He looks simple and good and sensitive.'

His bride, Anne Becher, was connected with an old Bengal civilian family, noted for the tenderness of its women. Perhaps the two most touching stories, carved on the Calcutta gravestones of the last century, are those on the tombs of her kinsman, Richard Becher, and his young wife. They shared in the expulsion of the English at the time of the Black Hole, June 1756, and in the miseries of the fever-stricken refuge in the delta waiting for deliverance. During that long-drawn-out agony they watched over a dying child. On December 14, Admiral Watson's fleet hove in sight; but exactly a fortnight before it dropped anchor at Fulta, Richard and Charlotte Becher had buried their infant.

The poor mother, herself but a girl of eighteen, never got over her sorrow. In 1757 she began to fade away. Next year Warren Hastings writes to her husband, 'greatly concerned to hear that Mrs. Becher's indisposition has increased,' and begging him to send her for change of air to Mrs. Hastings' house in the country. 'After suffering with patience a long illness occasioned by grief for the death of an only daughter,' says her epitaph, they laid her three years later in the same churchyard that contains the graves of Charnock, the founder, and Admiral Watson, the deliverer, of Calcutta.

The inscription on her husband's tomb is an even more pathetic one. Richard Becher arrived in Calcutta as a Writer in 1743. Rising through the various grades of the Company's service as Factor, Junior Merchant, and Senior Merchant, he had reached the rank of Fourth in the Bengal Council and Chief of Dacca at the time of the Black Hole, 1756. In the following year he returned with the survivors of the English to Calcutta, leaving his little daughter in her grave amid the swamps of the delta, and bringing back his sorely stricken wife. Like the other chief servants of the Company, he received a public donation of £27,000 from the new Nawab, by whom we superseded the prince under whose orders our countrymen had perished in the Black Hole. But unlike several of his colleagues, Richard Becher took no private gift, nor did the searching scrutiny of Parliament discover any sums, whether avowed or unavowed, accepted by him in the various subsequent revolutions and changes of native rulers.

During those years, while a handful of Englishmen were winning Plassey and creating an empire for the British nation in India, the Court of Directors was split into bitter factions. The party hostile to Clive, or envious of his success, having got the upper hand, vented its ill-humour in acrimonious despatches to Bengal. We saw how, in the previous century, the Court rewarded Charnock for his splendid defence which saved the English from extinction in Bengal [1], by telling him that—'it was not your wit or contrivance, but God Almighty's good providence, which hath always graciously superintended the affairs of the Company.' Clive was not a worn-out old man like Charnock, and he frankly expressed his indignation. On December 29, 1759, he and his Council remonstrated in very plain terms.

'Permit us to say,' runs their despatch, 'that the diction of your letter is most unworthy [of] yourselves and us, in whatever relation considered, either as master to servants or gentlemen to gentlemen.

[1] Ante, p. 44.

Mere inadvertences and casual neglects have been treated in such language and sentiments as nothing but the most glaring and premeditated frauds could warrant. . . . Faithful to little purpose, if the breath of scandal has power to blow away in one hour the merits of many years' service.'

Clive left Bengal in the following February, 1760, and was temporarily succeeded as Governor by his second in Council, Holwell, the hero and historian of the Black Hole. The Court of Directors, having no longer to deal with the conqueror of Plassey, took their revenge on his Council who together with Clive had signed the despatch. A full year afterwards, on January 21, 1761, they wrote to the Governor of Bengal: 'We do positively order and direct that immediately upon the receipt of this letter, all those persons remaining in the Company's service who signed the said letter of the 29th December . . . be dismissed from the Company's service.' Holwell and Richard Becher were the two chief signatories.

Holwell had already applied for leave to quit the Company's service owing to the 'many unmerited marks of resentment which I have lately received from the present Court of Directors.' On Richard Becher, who after eighteen years' service had made no considerable fortune, the blow fell.

Holwell retired at the age of fifty, to enjoy thirty-eight years of literary and social distinction in England. Several of his works may be read with pleasure at this day; his narrative of the Black Hole is a masterpiece of realism which will live to all time. Voltaire singled him out among the English Company's servants for his devotion to Eastern learning: 'Un homme qui n'a voyagé que pour s'instruire,' 'who has learned the language alike of the modern and ancient Brahmans, and translated sublime pieces from the earliest works in their sacred language.' 'These things,' continued Voltaire, 'are more worthy of the study of the wise man than the quarrels of dealers about muslins and dyed stuffs.'

Richard Becher's lot was very different. Dismissed the service in 1761, he remained out of employ for six years. But the necessities of the Company compelled the Court of Directors to swallow their angry words. Lord Clive returned as Governor of Bengal in 1765. Richard Becher, designated by him as one of the men to carry on his great task, was reappointed to the Bengal Council in 1767. He held that high office during the first years of Thackeray's grandfather in Calcutta, and was promoted in 1769 to be Resident at the Court of Murshidabad, with control, so far as we then ventured to interfere, of the revenue administration of Bengal.

Richard Becher will ever deserve honour as almost the only Englishman who, amid misrepresentation and calumny, strove to grapple with the great famine of 1770. What one man could do for the Province throughout its agony he accomplished. But no one felt more bitterly than himself the feebleness of the State relief, and his was the pen that awakened the conscience of his countrymen. Any effective dealing with famine was impossible under the divided control, half native, half English, which still prevailed in Bengal. In the words of the Indian proverb, it was watering the top of a tree whose roots were cut. Richard Becher got small thanks for his labours. Yet a century afterwards his letters and Consultations, as Resident at Murshidabad, fired me with admiration when a young Assistant Magistrate. They led to the attempt, in my *Annals of Rural Bengal*, to explain for the first time the true meaning of an Indian famine.

In 1774 Richard Becher retired to England with a competence after thirty-one years of service. He was a man, by the common consent of his fellow-men, absolutely pure-handed in the highest offices, ending with that next to the Governorship of Bengal. During seven years in England he had the happiness to see his boys grow into manhood. It was his sole reward in life. He lost his little fortune in trying to help a friend, and was charitably allowed to re-enter the Company's service at the age of sixty. They gave him a compassionate appointment as head of the Calcutta mint, together with nominations to the Bengal Civil Service for his sons, Richard and John. He brought out the two lads with him in the autumn of 1781. The youths, after long but not distinguished Indian careers, lived on in comfort in England till 1830 and 1846. The old man could not forget that he had been second only to the Governor, and died after one year of subordinate office.

The inscription on his Calcutta tombstone, in spite of some mortuary magniloquence, perhaps best tells the tale. For it speaks the feeling of his countrymen in Bengal at the time of his death. After recording his services, the honourable modesty of his fortune, and his return to England in 1774, it concludes: 'By nature open, liberal and compassionate: unpractised in guile and not suspecting it in others, to prop the declining credit of a friend he was led to put his all to the hazard, and fell a victim to his own benevolence. After a short pause and agonizing conflict, bound by domestic claims to fresh exertions, in 1781 he returned to the scene of his earlier efforts. But the vigour of life was past and . . . in the hopeless efforts to re-erect the fortunes of his family, under the pang of disappointment and the pressure of the climate, a worn mind and debilitated body sank to rest. An unerring wisdom ordained that his reward should not be of this world. Nov. 17, 1782.'

I wonder if Thackeray had that sad story of his mother's kinsman in mind, when he touched off, with so tender a pathos, Colonel Newcome's loss of fortune in old age? Colonel Newcome is indeed a character made up of many simples. There is in it, as we have seen, perhaps something of Thackeray's grand-uncle and guardian Moore, something of the chivalrous cousin Sir Richmond Shakespear, but perhaps also something of the poor old Richard Becher who lies in the South Park Street Cemetery, Calcutta. Happy the family which could count several members as the original of Colonel Newcome!

Richard Becher, notwithstanding his later misfortunes, founded an Indian connexion scarcely less powerful, or less widely spread, than that which derives from the elephant-hunting Thackeray of Sylhet. I have a manuscript record of no fewer than fifteen Bechers in India during the half-century after Richard's return thither in 1781. The *India List* for 1893 still showed four Bechers and four Thackerays in the services, besides many under other names through the female descent.

It was into this great Bengal family that Richmond Thackeray married. In 1779 John Harman Becher, a kinsman of the above Richard, arrived in Calcutta as a Writer. His career was cut short in his eighteenth year of service, and, after struggling against ill-health for three more years, he died in India in 1800. He left a little daughter, who grew into a beautiful girl of seventeen. This young lady, according to the Calcutta Old Cathedral register, Richmond Thackeray married on October 13, 1810. On July 18, 1811, their son, William Makepeace, the future novelist, was born at Calcutta. Five months later Richmond Thackeray was appointed Collector of the extensive District lying around the capital, then considered one of the prizes of the Bengal Service.

The young couple merely moved a mile out to their official residence in the suburbs, without any break in their Calcutta social life. The Collector's house at Alipur, which now became their home, was the country lodge of Sir Philip Francis in the last century: the 'villa inter paludes' where he held his weekly symposiums. The same house, with a wing and an upper story added, remains the official residence of the Collector of that District.

In it Richmond Thackeray spent the remaining four years of his life. His work was thenceforth confined to the routine of an old-established District, for a time supplemented by duty in Calcutta.

In him centered the whole internal administration of a tract of two thousand square miles, with a population now exceeding one and a half millions, exclusive of Calcutta and its suburbs. Besides this settled area, a wide unsurveyed region of forest and swamp, through which the Bengal rivers merge into the sea, then formed part of his jurisdiction. Thackeray had thus the capital of India at one end of his District and a no-man's-land of creeks and jungle, inhabited only by tigers, deer, crocodile, and the few remnants of the old river-pirates, at the other.

Although his duties partook more of a daily round than in his previous frontier Districts, they were sufficiently numerous. He supervised the collection of the revenue, exceeding £100,000 a year, from the land and other sources. He was a criminal judge and a judge in land-suits, both of first instance and in appeal; and as head of the police responsible for the peace of the District and the prevention of crime. But these by no means exhausted his multifarious functions.

The Collector of a Bengal District does in his local sphere all that the Home Secretary superintends in England, and a great deal more. For he is the representative of a paternal and not of a constitutional Government. Roads, ferries, bridges, river-floods, jails, lunatics, child-landowners, State pensioners and wards, education, epidemics, dispensaries, payments for killing snakes and tigers, cattle-disease, municipalities, the reclamation of waste lands, the introduction of new crops, village-pounds, the embankment and the deepening of water-channels, the changing prospects of the harvest, and measures to relieve distress caused by failure of the rains, form a few of the matters with which he has to deal. If some of them have developed since Richmond Thackeray's time, others were more exclusively concentrated in his hands.

Richmond Thackeray was a great road-maker. On coming to Calcutta in 1807 he had observed the inferior material, broken brick or lumps of burnt clay, used for the streets; and contrasted them with the durable roads metalled from the iron strata and nodular limestone in his old District, Birbhum. He accordingly urged the advantages of the Birbhum 'gravel' on the Committee for improving the town; and had samples sent down for their inspection. The city was then beginning to push its way out towards the south, and his settlement of the suburban hamlets over eighty years ago forms a landmark in the history of Calcutta.

On September 13, 1815, Richmond Thackeray died; aged thirty-two years, ten months and twenty-three days, says his tombstone. This would make his birthday October 21, 1782, instead of September 1, 1781, as stated in the Family Book (ante, p. 141). They laid him in the North Park Street Cemetery: on the other side of the road from the graveyard in which his wife's kinsman, Richard Becher, sleeps off the sorrows of his old age.

You walk along the north side of Park Street, passing a couple of closed burial-grounds, until you come to a padlocked gate of a third cemetery, labelled with municipal precision No. 28, when last I visited it. After a delay, you may get the key from the doorkeeper of a fourth graveyard, just opposite. Enter the gate, and turn to the left, until, by a coarse path of broken brick, lined with blackened and ruinous sepulchres, you reach the western wall. Then go on twenty paces, and you are at Richmond Thackeray's tomb.

It is a brick monument consisting of a squat column rising from an oblong base. The plaster, when I saw it, was scaling off, and the platform showed signs of decay. Yet the whole was in good preservation compared with some of the hideous ruins around. Near it on the right rose a poor *khatar* tree, its laurel-like leaves very dusty. A toddy palm of an equally sordid growth stood three graves off on the left. But the sunset poured a golden flood over the wall from the west on the shrivelled foliage and the forgotten dead.

At the other side of the red path rises an imposing mausoleum to a boy civilian, Thomas Henry Graham, 'who fell gloriously,' says his inscription, 'in an action between the Honourable East India Company's ship *Kent* and a French privateer at the mouth of the Ganges, on October 7, 1800—the day on which he completed the sixteenth year of his age.' We have seen how another boy hero, 'Billy' Speke, gave his life also at the age of sixteen on the earlier *Kent* which carried Admiral Watson's flag. In 1798, two years before young Graham's death on his way to join his first appointment, Richmond Thackeray sailed for India, also in his sixteenth year. After seventeen years' service they buried him opposite Graham with a tribute to his worth as a public officer, 'a son, a brother, a husband, a father, and a friend.'

To the same graveyard had been borne, a few years earlier, amid the boom of minute guns and the pomp of military honours, Colonel Ball, Adjutant-General of the Bengal Army, glorious from the campaigns of Lord Lake. Not far off rests the soldier-political, Colonel Achilles Kirkpatrick, who imposed the treaty on the Nizam which demolished the French power, and made our own supreme, in Southern India. Among sailors are the once famous Ambrose Kepling, and Captain Cudbert Thornhill, a sort of eighteenth-century Sinbad, honourably mentioned by Bruce the Abyssinian traveller, and at whose death 'all the vessels in the harbour, both foreign and British, joined the Honourable Company's Marine in lowering their colours half mast.' Here also sleeps the good doctor, Surgeon William Pitt Muston, the inventor or improver of the army dooley, who, after a life of humanity, obtained a slow redress against injustice from the Court of Directors, but returned to India only to hear of the fall of his gallant son, and to sink broken-hearted into the grave.

The old civil service is well represented by a Shore, son of the civilian Governor-General Lord Teignmouth the real framer of the Permanent Settlement of Bengal; by a Halked, son of the civilian codifier of Hindu Law; by Peter Speke, long a ruling voice in the Supreme Council; and by a multitude of once potent civilian names, including a Groeme, an Udny, a couple of Barwells, and of course a Chichely Plowden. The page of the Obituary which begins with the inscription to Richmond Thackeray ends with one from the tomb of Mrs. Arthur Grote in the same graveyard —two Bengal civilian families destined to perpetual honour.

Richmond Thackeray left an only son, the future novelist, just four years old. The young mother, herself only twenty-three, found a home with her relatives in India, and to the grief of widowhood had soon to add the sorrow of separation from her child. This was in 1817. Forty-four years afterwards Thackeray, in one of his Roundabout Papers, described a similar parting, 'remembering in long long distant days,' he says, 'such a ghaut or river-stair at Calcutta; and a day when down those steps, to a boat which was in waiting, came two children whose mothers remained on shore.' The two children were Thackeray and his cousin, Sir Richmond Shakespear.

The beautiful young mother was the dream of his childhood. 'He drew me your house in Calcutta,' wrote Grandmamma Becher soon after Thackeray's arrival in England, 'not omitting the monkey looking out of the window, and black Betty at the top drying the towels.' This was a postscript to Thackeray's first extant letter to his mother at the age of six and a half years. Her engagement to Captain Carmichael Smyth, afterwards Superintendent of Addiscombe, never loosened the early bond. In that first letter the child sends his love to the Captain, 'and tell him he must bring you home to your affectionate little son.'

It was the mother's influence that remained with him through life. Divided by half the world the child clung to her memory: the separation was followed by years of tender reunion which ended only with his death. When suffering from the tyrant of a private school, 'I remember,' he wrote forty years afterwards, 'kneeling by my little bed at night, and saying, "Pray God I may dream of my mother."' The public schoolboy at Charterhouse wrote almost daily to her a sort of journal. For her the gay young man at Cambridge and Weimar found leisure to compile the most delightful pictorial epistles. On her second widowhood his house became her home. His one surviving daughter bears her name. The shadow of a great domestic sorrow settled heavily on his prime: he was cut off before he reached the honours of old age. But the tenderness of that beautiful mother went with him through his whole life. He was her only child; and the same gentle eyes that filled with joy when he was born wept with sorrow when he was laid under the sod. On the first anniversary of his death she followed him to her own grave.

When I knew her,' writes the family chronicler, 'she was old, and her hair—of a lovely whiteness—contrasted with her fine eyebrows. There was a look of great refinement and nobleness about her.' 'Walk into the drawing-room,' writes Thackeray of the home which he made for his mother's evening of life. 'There sits an old lady of more than fourscore years, serene and kind, and as beautiful in her age now as in her youth. She is as simple as if she had never had any flattery to dazzle her. Can that have been anything but a good life which, after more than eighty years of it was spent, is so calm?'

An influence of another kind on Thackeray's character was his descent, through his grandmother Amelia Richmond-Webb, from the noble Constables of Richmond and Lords of Burton. His father perpetuated their name of Richmond in the last century, as his son-in-law does in the present one. The great novelist used their crest as his signet ring: a coronet transfixed with three darts, from one of which fall three drops of blood, in combination with a monogram designed by himself. Thackeray had the genuine pride of birth, the absence of which is so often covered over by the mixture of ostentation and meanness which he branded as snobbery. His love of ancient lineage was no mean admiration of mean things, but a noble admiration of noble deeds. He gave his grandmother's name, Amelia, to the lady whom he intended to be the purest of his early female creations. In his historical masterpiece of *Esmond* he makes his famous relative, General Webb, stand out as he does in the tapestry at Blenheim. Indeed the prominence of the burly brigadier forms perhaps a little bit of wrong perspective in that great novel.

But if the grandmother's ancestry touched his imagination with the wand of romance, he derived the strong fibre of his nature from the grandfather's side. During a hundred years his branch of the Thackerays had been a landless people belonging to the strictly professional class. Of sixty-nine kinsmen and collaterals whose career I have been able to trace, twenty-four entered the army or navy, nineteen were churchmen, nine were barristers, eight were Indian civilians, seven were medical men, two were Eton masters. Every Thackeray since the Archdeacon, nearly two hundred years ago, had to earn his living in some honourable profession: by his sword, tongue, or pen. In the generation immediately preceding the novelist, we have seen that at least four uncles and one aunt had literary gifts. Thackeray's genius was the flowering of a century and a half of family culture; a culture of which the beautiful after-efflorescence still blooms in *Old Kensington*, the *Story of Elizabeth*, and the *Village on the Cliff*.

Thackeray's robustness of character, his hatred of shams, his scorn of all things base, had their roots deep down in the manly life of the old Yorkshire moorland. The power of producing high-class mental work to order, when work must needs be done, came to him from a century of later ancestors who had made their bread by their brains. The loneliness and unsatisfied dim yearnings for love which each generation of Anglo-Indian children suffer, and the perpetual pathos of parting in our Indian life, have also left a touching record on his pages. 'Strong men alone on their knees,' he tells us, 'with streaming eyes and broken accents, implore heaven for those little ones who were prattling at their sides but a few hours since. Long after they are gone, careless and happy, recollections of the sweet past rise up and smite those who remain: the flowers they had planted in their little gardens, the toys they played with, the little vacant cribs they slept in as fathers' eyes looked blessings down on them.'

The clerical traditions of a family, with nineteen parsons among them, made Thackeray, quite apart from his intellectual convictions, the friend of true churchmen, and filled his imagination with the poetry of the rites of the Church. 'How should he who knows you,' he wrote, 'not respect you or your calling? May this pen never write a pennyworth again if it ever cast ridicule upon either.' His boyhood was solitary. For him, memory required a long vista to soften the harsh lines of his school years, and to etherealise the Slaughter House (Charter House) of his earlier novels into the Grey Friars, to which the three friends made their tender pilgrimage, and where the old colonel murmured his last *Adsum*. It is the recollection, however, of the chapel-service which makes the transformation complete. 'A plenty of candles lights up this chapel and this scene of age and youth and early memories, and pompous death. How solemn the well-remembered prayers are, here uttered again in the place where in childhood we used to hear them. How beautiful and decorous the rite:

how noble the ancient words of the supplications which the priest utters, and to which generations of fresh children, and troops of bygone seniors, have cried Amen.'

But the greatest single influence of Thackeray's life-work was still his mother. My earliest portrait of him is that of a little child clinging to his mother, her arm around his neck, and the father sitting close by. At any rate it is something that the best of Bengal civilian families in the last century furnished the mother of Thackeray. The lofty tenderness for women which he learned from that mother, he lavished on his wife until parted from her by her dark malady; it overflowed to his daughters, and breathes in his works. How exquisite the transition in the closing verse of his *White Squall*, when

> 'The harmless storm was ended,
> And as the sunrise splendid
> Came blushing o'er the sea;
> I thought, as day was breaking,
> My little girls were waking,
> And smiling, and making
> A prayer at home for me.'

In Lady Castlewood he runs up the whole gamut

of tenderness, from the subdued sentiment of the Cathedral scene on Esmond's return from the wars, to the high-strung scene of her presentation of him as head of the family to the Duke of Hamilton—one of not too many passages in which Thackeray cared to reach the sublime. In his lecture on Dean Swift what a picture of the Nemesis which avenges heartlessness to women! 'He was always alone, alone, and gnashing in the darkness, except when Stella's sweet smile came and shone on him. When that went, silence and utter night closed over him. An immense genius, an awful downfall and ruin.' 'A good woman,' he says elsewhere, 'is the loveliest flower that blooms under heaven, and we look with love and wonder upon its silent grace, its pure fragrance, its delicate bloom of beauty.' 'Lucky is he in life who knows a few such women! A kind providence of Heaven it was that sent us such, and gave us to admire that touching and wonderful spectacle of innocence and love and beauty.'

How would he have chosen that this chronicle of the strenuous lives of his countrymen in India—sometimes unloved, often ill-requited, generally cut short—should end?

'Canst thou, O friendly reader,' he asks, 'count upon the fidelity of an artless heart or tender or two, and reckon among the blessings which Heaven hath bestowed on thee the love of faithful women? Purify thine own heart, and try to make it worthy of theirs. All the prizes of life are nothing compared to that one. All the rewards of ambition, wealth, pleasure, only vanity and disappointment grasped at greedily and fought for fiercely, and over and over again found worthless by the weary winners.' It was the mother of Thackeray that taught him to think thus of women. Her kindred lie amid the dismal sepulchres of Calcutta graveyards. But her nobler nature did not perish. It is immortal in the immortality of the manliest and tenderest man of letters of our age.

INDEX

A.

Agnew, Vans, tablet to his memory in Calcutta Cathedral, quoted, 59.

Anville: see **D'Anville.**

Aylmer, Rose, daughter of Lord Aylmer, and one of Landor's early loves, 59, 60; her death in Calcutta and her tombstone, 59, 60; Landor's elegy on her, 61.

B.

Ball, Colonel, 174.

Barwell, Richard, 15; his duel with Sir John Clavering, 17; Francis' opinion of him, 25.

Batson, Mr., 24.

Becher, Anne, wife of Richmond Thackeray, 159–61; 169; birth of her son William Makepeace (the novelist), 169; second marriage to Captain Carmichael Smyth, 176; her influence on her son, 176-7, 182–4; her death, 177.

Becher, John, 166.

Becher, John Harman, 168–9.

Becher, Richard, his life and misfortunes, 160–6; his death, 166–7.

Bengal Obituary, The, 56, 62, 175.

Bentinck, Lord William, Governor of Madras, 124–6, 128–9.

Bosworth Smith, his *Life of Lord Lawrence*, 58.

Bruce, the Abyssinian traveller, 174.

Burke, Edmund, 106.

C.

Calcutta, the grave-yards of, 9, 13, 17, 18, 21, 23, 27–8, 32, 52–3, 59–62, 139, 140, 161, 167, 172–5; life in, 11, 12; founded by Job Charnock, 32, 38, 43–4, 47–8; rapid growth of, 49–50; its unhealthiness, 50; its earliest newspaper, 55.

Caraccioli's *Life of Clive*, 12.

Cartier, John, Governor of Bengal, 70, 73, 81–3.

Charnock, Job, founder of Calcutta, 32, 44, 48, 55, 85; previous career, 34-53; marriage, 34-5; his repeated attempts to settle at 'Cotton Mart Hamlet,' afterwards Calcutta, 41-5, 47-9; his unhappy old age, 50, 51; his death and burial in 1693, 51; his gravestone, 32, 52-3, 161; summary of his life and character, 51-2.

Clavering, General Sir John, 15, 17, 18.

Clevland, Augustus, 59.

Clive, Lord Robert, 27, 69, 70-1, 73, 79, 84-5, 143, 162-4.

Clive, Lord, Governor of Madras, 116.

College of Fort William, 142.

Congreve, Sir William, 108.

Coote, Sir Eyre, Commander-in-Chief in India, 24, 25.

Cotton Mart Hamlet or Cotton Thread Mart, a mud hamlet on the east bank of the river Hugli, the site of the present Calcutta, 39-44, 47-50.

D.

Dacca in the last century, 74.

Dalhousie, Lord, quoted, 140.

D'Anville, 77.

De Richmond: see **Richmond.**

E.

East India Company, 67; Bengal granted to it by the Mughal Emperor in 1765, 68-9; its investment, its servants and their private trade, 71-3, 84; its retrenchments, 79-80.

Elphinstone, Hon. Mountstuart, 156.

Englishman, The, Calcutta newspaper, 114-5.

Evans, John, Chaplain to the East India Company and private trader, afterwards Bishop of Bangor and finally of Armagh, 47, 49, 52.

F.

Foley, George, his grave in South Park Street Cemetery, 61.

Francis, Sir Philip, 10, 11; his identity with 'Junius,' 14; leaves England in chagrin and arrives in Calcutta in 1774, 14; his colleagues in the Indian Council, 14, 15; his resolve to become Governor of Bengal, 15; his intrigues to ruin Warren Hastings, 15, 16, 92; his schemes defeated, 16; his duel with Warren Hastings, 21-2; returns to England, 1780, 22; death in 1818, 23; his libel on Sir Eyre Coote, 24-5; various references to, 68, 106, 169.

G.

Graham, Thomas Henry, his grave in Calcutta, 173.

Grand, George, 68.

Grant, John Peter, 114.
Grote, Mrs. Arthur, 175.

H.

Halked, 175.
Hamilton, Surgeon William, cures the Emperor of Delhi and obtains privileges for the English Company, 32–3; ingratitude of the Directors, 33; his death in 1717 and burial in Calcutta, 34; his gravestone, 32, 34, 53.
Harris, Mr. James, Chief of the Council of Dacca in 1771, 81–2; marries Henrietta Thackeray in 1772, 82; their return to England and life there, 82–3; his death, 83.
Hastings, Warren, 13, 15, 71, 82, 85, 89, 92, 160; parentage, 19, 20; long conflict with Sir Philip Francis, 16, 17; duel with Francis, 21, 22; death in 1818, 23.
Heath, Captain, 45–6.
Hicky's *Bengal Gazette* (1780), the earliest Calcutta newspaper, 55.
Holland, Lord, 106.
Holwell, hero and historian of 'the Black Hole of Calcutta,' is dismissed from the East India Company's service, 163; his literary works, 164.

I.

Impey, Sir Elijah, 63.
Inglis, Sir Hugh, a trader at Dacca, his help to the Thackerays, 111, 112.
Ives, Dr., surgeon on Admiral Watson's flag-ship, quoted, 28–31.

J.

Junius: see **Sir Philip Francis.**

K.

Kaye, Sir James William, quoted, 147.
Kepling, Ambrose, 174.
Kilpatrick, Major, his death and burial in 1757, 28.
Kirkpatrick, Colonel Achilles, 174.
Kukis, a hill-tribe, 90.

L.

Landor, Walter Savage, his love for and elegy on Rose Aylmer, 59–61.
Leith, John Farley, 114.
Lindsay, Hon. Robert, son of the Earl of Balcarres, Resident or 'Collector' of Sylhet in 1778, 86; his administration of Sylhet and private trade, 86–90, 92, 93.
Low, General Sir John, British Resident in Oudh; his marriage to Augusta Shakespear, 147.

M.

Macaulay, Lord, his story of Warren Hastings' parentage, 12; proofs of its falseness, 19,

20; his essays set up at *The Englishman* Press, Calcutta, 115.

Markham, Sir Clements, quoted, 78, 81.

Milton, John, his last descendant died in Madras, 9.

Minto, Lord, 159.

Moira, Lord, 148–9.

Monson, Colonel, 15; his illness and death, 18.

Monson, Lady Anne, her ancestors, 19; her whist-parties in Calcutta, 19; her slander of Warren Hastings, 19; her death, 20; and grave, 18.

Moore, Mr. Peter, 100–2; his marriage to Sarah Richmond Webb and life in England, 102-4; his parliamentary career, 105–7; his speculations, ruin and death, 106–8; his guardianship of his great-nephew, the novelist, 109–111.

Munro, Sir Thomas, 117; his settlement of the 'Ceded Provinces,' 117–121; his friendship for William Thackeray, 121, 123, 130; Governor of Madras in 1820, 133; his tribute to William Thackeray's memory, 134; death of his nephew, 136.

Muston, Surgeon William Pitt, 174.

N.

North Park Street Graveyard, Calcutta; Richard Becher buried in 1782, 167; Richmond Thackeray in 1815, 172-3; Thomas Henry Graham in 1800, 173; also Colonel Ball, Colonel Achilles Kirkpatrick, Ambrose Kepling, Captain Cudbert Thornhill, Surgeon William Pitt Muston, 174; Shore, Halked, Peter Speke, Groeme, Udny, Chichely Plowden, two Barwells, and Mrs. Arthur Grote, 175.

O.

Orme, 51, 57.

P.

Park, Mungo, 77.

Park Street Cemeteries, Calcutta: see **North Park Street** and **South Park Street Graveyards.**

Pearse, Colonel, Warren Hastings' second in his duel with Francis, 21–3.

Pigot, Lord, Governor of Madras, 24.

Plowden, Chichely, 175.

R.

Ray, Miss, 68.

Rennell, Major James, 75–7; death in 1830 and burial in Westminster Abbey, 77; narrow escapes, 78–81; Surveyor-General of Bengal, 79; his opinion of Clive's retrenchments, 79-80; marriage to Jane Thackeray, 78, 81; their married life in Bengal, 95, 96; and in England, 103; his position as a geographer, 104; reference to, 140.

Richmond, original name of a family claiming descent from the De Richmonds, changed in the fifteenth century, through marriage, to **Richmond-Webb**, 97–8, 100.

Richmond-Webb: see **Richmond**; also **Webb**.

Ritchie, Mrs. Anne, daughter of the novelist, 159, 180.

Ritter, 77.

Rollin, his *Ancient History*, quoted, 80.

Russell, Sir Henry, Chief Justice of Bengal, and **Lady Russell**, 60, 63.

S.

Saint John's Churchyard, Calcutta; Admiral Watson buried there, 27, 161; also 'Billy' Speke, 28, 32; Job Charnock, the founder of Calcutta, 32, 161; Surgeon Hamilton, 32; Charlotte Becher, 161; monument to twelve officers who fell in a conflict with the Rohillas, 32.

Sandwich, Lord, 68.

Shakespear, Augusta, her marriage to General Low, 147.

Shakespear, Colonel John Dowdeswell, 147.

Shakespear, John Talbot, marriage to Emily Thackeray, 146, 147; death, 149.

Shakespear, Colonel Sir Richmond, 147–8.

Sheridan, Richard Brinsley, his death and burial, 106–7.

Shore, a son of the Governor-General, Lord Teignmouth; his grave, 175.

Smith, Bosworth, 58.

Smyth, Captain Carmichael, second husband of Anne Becher, 176.

South Park Street Graveyard, Calcutta; opened in 1767, 13; Sir John Clavering buried there, 17; also Colonel Monson in 1776 and his wife, Lady Anne, 18; Colonel Pearse in 1789, 21; Rose Aylmer in 1800, 60; George Foley, 61; Richard Becher, 167, 172; and many Bayleys, 62.

Speke, 'Billy,' son of Captain Henry Speke, and midshipman on Admiral Watson's flagship; father and son both struck during the capture of Chandarnagar, 29; heroic fortitude and death of 'Billy,' 29–31.

Speke, Peter, 175.

Stocqueler, J. H., 114.

T.

Talleyrand, Princesse de, 68.

Thackerays, The, a great Indian family, their history, 64–7.

Thackeray, Augusta, sister to Richmond Thackeray; goes out to him in India, 146; her marriage to Mr. Elliot, 147.

Thackeray, Charles, youngest son of W. M. Thackeray and uncle of the novelist; born 1794, 113; his life in India as a barrister, and journalist, 114; his death, 114.

Thackeray, Emily, sister to Richmond Thackeray; goes out to him in India, 146; her marriage to John Talbot Shakespear, 146; her children, 147–8; her death, 149.

Thackeray, The Rev. Francis, son of W. M. Thackeray and uncle of the novelist; his life and writings, 112, 113.

Thackeray, Henrietta, sister of W. M. Thackeray and great-aunt of the novelist; her home in Dacca with her brother, 75; her marriage to J. Harris in 1772, 82; her life and widowhood in England, 83, 102; her descendants, 83.

Thackeray, Jane, eldest sister to W. M. Thackeray, 75, 78; her marriage to James Rennell, 78. See **Rennell**.

Thackeray, Richmond, born 1781, second son of W. M. Thackeray and father of the novelist; his education, 141; his life in India, 141–3, 145–6, 149, 150, 152–9, 168–71; his marriage to Anne Becher, 159, 169; birth of his son William Makepeace (the novelist), 169; his death in 1815 and burial in Calcutta, 172.

Thackeray, St. John, son of W. M. Thackeray, uncle of the novelist; enters the Madras Civil Service in 1809, 135; his life in India and gallant death in 1824, 136.

Thackeray, Dr. Thomas, great-grandfather of the novelist Head-master of Harrow, 66–7.

Thackeray, Thomas, Lieutenant, eighth son of W. M. and Amelia Thackeray, and uncle of the novelist; his career and heroic death, 137–9.

Thackeray, Webb, third son of W. M. Thackeray and uncle of the novelist, 100; enters the Madras Civil Service as writer in 1806, 135; his death, 135.

Thackeray, William, born 1778, eldest son of W. M. Thackeray, 116–7; appointed assistant to Sir Thomas Munro in 1800, 116; their friendship, 121–3; member of the Board of Revenue in 1806, 126; Lord W. Bentinck's opinion of him, 127; his 'Report' of 1807, 131; Chief Secretary to the Government in 1810, 133; illness, 133; President of the Board of Revenue in 1820, 134; death in 1823, 134; tributes to his memory, 134.

Thackeray, William Makepeace, son of Dr. Thomas Thackeray and grandfather of the novelist; birth and education, 67; voyage to India, 68; arrival in Calcutta in 1766,

69; his five years there, 70–3; Factor and Fourth in Council at Dacca in 1771, 73; sends for his two sisters, their marriages in India, 75–83; private trading, 83–5; 'Collector' of Sylhet, 85–9; his army-contract for elephants, 91–2; administration of Sylhet, 93–5; Third in Council at Dacca in 1774, 95; marriage with Amelia Richmond Webb in 1776, 98; return to England and home at Hadley, 98, 100, 102–5; his whole official pay, 99; his children, 100, 105, 112, 115; death in 1813, 105.

Thackeray, William Makepeace (the novelist); his parents, 159, 168; birth at Calcutta, 168; death and funeral of his father, 64, 108, 172; is sent to England at the age of six, 109, 175; visits to his guardian and grand-uncle, Mr. Peter Moore, at Hadley, 109; his fortune, 109, 110; his mother's influence, 176–7, 182–4; letters to his mother, 176–7; re-marriage of his mother, 176; school-days at Charterhouse, 176–7; studies at Cambridge and Weimar, 177; his crest and ancestors, 178–9; his character, 179, 180; his wife, 182; his views of women, 182–4.

Thornhill, Captain Cudbert, 174.

V.

Vansittart, Governor of Bengal, 76.

Verelst, Governor of Bengal, 69.

W.

Walckenaer, Baron, 77.

Watson, Admiral, relieves Calcutta after the Black Hole, 26–7; captures Hugli and Chandarnagar, 27; dies and is buried in St. John's Churchyard, 27; his signature forged and his name calumniated, 27–8.

Webb, Amelia Richmond, daughter of Col. Richmond Webb, 97; her marriage to William Makepeace Thackeray in 1776, 98; her death, 105.

Webb, General John Richmond, distinguished during Marlborough's campaigns, 98.

Webb, Lieutenant-Colonel Richmond, father of W. M. Thackeray's wife, Amelia; his life summarised, 97; origin of the family, 97; death of his son, 100; his character and advice to his son, 103.

Webb, Sarah Richmond, eldest daughter of Colonel Richmond Webb and sister to Amelia, 102; her marriage to Mr. Peter Moore, 102.

Wellesley, Marquis of, 143, 145.

Woodward, John, 66.